The Junior College

THE LIBRARY OF EDUCATION

A Project of The Center for Applied Research in Education, Inc.

G. R. Gottschalk, Director

Categories of Coverage

I	II	III
Curriculum and Teaching	Administration, Organization, and Finance	Psychology for Educators

IV	V	VI
History, Philosophy, and Social Foundations	Professional Skills	Educational Institutions

The Junior College

JAMES W. REYNOLDS

Professor and Consultant
in Junior College Education
The University of Texas

The Center for Applied Research in Education, Inc.
New York

Foreword

For a half-century the junior college has been one of the most rapidly growing units in the American school system, and its growth is now transforming our pattern of institutional organization. At the same time that the number of junior colleges and their enrollments have been rapidly increasing, the ways of incorporating them in the school system and the variation of practices within the units of the system have multiplied. A compact overview and appraisal of these developments has long been needed. This is provided in *The Junior College*.

The author is not one who has come lately to hear about the junior college and now has the urge to transmit an amateur's enthusiasm to its promotion. His contact with the field began as a teacher in and administrative head of a junior college. Next, he focused his graduate studies on the field of the junior college, under subvention from the General Education Board. Since then he has had a distinguished university career in teaching, research, and consultation —all in relation to the junior college. From this seasoned background he has extracted a brief, yet comprehensive, treatise that will provide an understanding of the movement for the many who are now exploring it for the first time, as well as an enlightening reorientation for teachers, administrators, and others connected with junior colleges.

LEONARD V. KOOS

The Junior College

James W. Reynolds

The junior college, one of the youngest members in the family of institutions of higher education in the United States is also the most rapidly growing member of that family. The number of new institutions of the junior college type founded in the past few decades exceeds the number of all other kinds of new institutions combined. In the years since World War II the percentage of increase in total enrollments of junior colleges has consistently been larger than that of any other major category of institutions of higher education. It is fitting that a volume in the Library of Education should be devoted to this interesting and striking development in American higher education.

Dr. Reynolds treats various aspects of the junior college in the United States, using the historical approach to describe and explain its present functions and operations. He accurately classifies junior colleges into the two major types that are characteristic of all higher education in the United States—the publicly controlled and the privately controlled. Under each of these major classes he treats the distinct sub-categories, such as the state junior college, the local public junior college, the junior college that is maintained as a branch of a university, the church-related junior college, the independent private institution, and the proprietary college.

Throughout the book Dr. Reynolds consistently refers to the institution as the *junior college,* its older and more general designation. The newer term, *community college,* is referred to only briefly, with the explanation that it is included under the sub-category of local public junior college.

The volume on *The Junior College* is parallel in the Library of Education series to other books on various kinds of educational institutions, such as *The Municipal University* by Carlson, *State*

Colleges and Universities by Wahlquist and Thornton, *The Church-Related College* by Wicke, *The Smaller Liberal Arts College* by Mayhew, and *The Technical Institute* by Graney. Similar treatment of other levels of the American educational system will be found in *Trends and Issues in Secondary Education* by Douglass, *The Junior High School* by Brimm, and *Elementary Education* by Lambert.

This book on the junior college should be of great interest to all who are concerned with current problems in American education. In those communities which have a junior college, there might well be interest in measuring the local institution against the norms presented by Dr. Reynolds. Throughout the country many communities are considering the establishment of new junior colleges; Dr. Reynolds provides much valuable information and advice regarding the features that characterize a successful institution of this kind. It may be expected that, in areas where the junior college is not well known, educational leaders may be stimulated by Dr. Reynolds' book to begin a study of how local needs might be met by such an institution. The book deserves a wide audience.

JOHN DALE RUSSELL
Content Editor

Contents

The Junior College

CHAPTER I

The Junior College in Higher Education

The Growth of the Junior College

The colleges and universities of the United States have been confronted since the end of World War II with many novel policy problems. Among them, one remains constant: how to accommodate the phenomenal increase in the number of applicants seeking admission.

Three factors are responsible for this increase. First, subsidies for education were provided to the veterans of World War II and, later, to veterans of the Korean Conflict. Although some veterans devoted the money from their G.I. Bill of Rights to educational activities below college level, many thousands used the money to defray expenses in college. Second, there has been a marked increase in the number of boys and girls who remain in high school through graduation, then seek admission to college. Third, the products of the large upswing in the birth rate—the so-called war babies—have reached college age and have increased the number of students seeking admission into college.

The same post-World War II period which has seen the great increase in the number of college students has also witnessed an almost inconceivable advance in technology. The substitution of machine power for man power, already evident before this period, has been accelerated at a tremendous pace. Automation has spread to all phases of human activity: the home, industry, agriculture, business, and the professions.

Power generation, which had moved at a snail's pace from water power to steam, from steam to internal combustion, electricity, and heat, has moved rapidly to experimentation with nuclear fission and fusion.

Electronic principles have been applied to the development of mass communication media. As a result, events on any part of the

1

planet become known intimately on all parts of the earth in a matter of seconds after they occur.

The earth-bound limits of man's movements have yielded to the results of explorations into outer space. More and more, people have ceased thinking only in terms of the planet on which they live.

Medical science, too, has made rapid strides during this period. Man's normal life expectancy has been prolonged materially. Dread diseases have been conquered, and the possibility of overcoming many killing and crippling ailments has been brought much closer to realization.

Technological progress has caused a near-revolution in the field of occupational opportunity. Many of the older occupations have become obsolete. The newer ones in the technical fields very often require longer periods of preservice preparation. The advantage once conferred by the high school diploma has decreased materially.

Colleges and universities have become more accessible to more people by the improvements in means of transportation and communication. This, combined with the increasing social pressure created by the growing proportion of college-educated people in the population, has caused a substantial upswing in the number of applicants for admission to colleges and universities.

The response of the policy-makers to the phenomenally increased demand for a college education was not uniform. Many public institutions of higher education increased their student facilities, and their enrollments—as compared to prewar days—assumed almost astronomical proportions. Others, many of them privately controlled and lacking the resources to expand, set enrollment limits and held to them by progressively raising their admission standards.

Public higher education in this country has traditionally been controlled by the several states. It was only natural that this pattern should prevail in the efforts to accommodate the constantly increasing numbers who sought admission to college. There was no uniformity among the states in the methods devised to meet the situation. Some states undertook to solve the problem through legislative action and through state boards of higher education and similar agencies. Others employed educational experts to conduct statewide studies, and to make recommendations for possible solutions.

One fairly widely adopted solution was the placing of greater reliance on that institution of higher education known as the *junior college*. Although junior colleges have existed in the United States for over a half-century, their nature was rather unfamiliar to people in all but a relatively small number of states. In brief, nontechnical terms, the junior college may be defined as an educational institution with a two-year instructional program designed for students who are high school graduates or of comparable maturity.

Advocates of increased reliance on the junior college were able to point out the advantages of such a solution to the problems of increasing demands for higher education. For example, the establishment of junior colleges is less expensive than that of four-year colleges. Moreover, the fact that these institutions are located in centers of population make them accessible to prospective students at a lower cost. Junior college students may live at home, thereby eliminating expenses for room and board. Another advantage that could be stressed was the junior college's established record of serving satisfactorily both transfer and terminal students. Abundant evidence existed to support these records.

As junior colleges increased in number in certain states, and as word of their existence spread to other states, public curiosity about their nature increased. This monograph undertakes to provide a comprehensive description of the junior college and to answer most of the questions to which that curiosity has given rise.

For the most part, this treatment will concern itself with the many facets of the junior college that are found in the postwar period. An understanding of these conditions, however, requires a relatively brief consideration of the growth and development of the junior college as an institution of higher education.

The Origin of the Junior College

Four patterns are easily discerned in the origin of junior colleges in the United States: (1) the upward extension of high schools or academies; (2) the transformation of many church-related colleges from four-year to two-year institutions; (3) the evolution of educational institutions initially intended to bring advantages to young people in rural areas; and (4) the creation of junior colleges by philanthropic groups or individuals. Although other patterns do exist, these four comprehend a majority of the junior colleges established in the early years of this century.

The upward extension of high schools and academies. As early as the mid-nineteenth century, some of the more perceptive scholars of higher education began to make a distinction between the first two years of the four-year undergraduate college and the last two. The freshman and sophomore years were devoted to courses that served as preparation for the more specialized studies of the junior and senior years. This distinction led some scholars to advocate the removal of the first two years from the college and their addition to the high school.

By the beginning of the twentieth century, a second force was added. In at least two sections of the country, the Midwest and California, the idea was being advanced that the high school should be lengthened by two additional years. The arguments in support of these pleas were not so much concerned with what was happening in the educational program of the college as it was with making possible two additional years of formal schooling for boys and girls while they remained at home.

It would be fruitless to argue that one or the other of these two forces was most responsible for the founding of the junior college as an upward extension of the high school. The significant point is that one junior college was established in Illinois in 1902 and another in California in 1910, and that these served as prototypes for many new institutions that were later established in the Midwest and in California.

The transformation of church-related colleges. The period following the end of the Civil War in 1865 marked the rise of a substantial number of new four-year colleges created by many of the Protestant denominations. Frequently, the desire of the founders to provide higher education in a religious environment exceeded their financial ability to maintain the new colleges. As a result, many of these colleges soon encountered serious financial problems. In many instances, the financial problems proved too serious to solve, and the colleges were closed. In other instances, the financial storm was weathered, and the colleges continued. In still other cases, however, the problems were solved through the simple device of transforming the four-year college into a junior college.

The specialized programs of the third and fourth years of the four-year college are much more expensive to maintain than the general program of the first two years. Specialized curriculums incur higher costs through such features as more complex laboratory equipment, larger library collections, and faculty members with doctorates. Moreover, the normal dropout rate in colleges is much higher during the first two years than it is during the last two. Thus, the higher cost of the upper-division program is distributed over a smaller number of students, so that the per-student cost of education is much higher in the upper division than it is in the lower division. This was the factor which dictated the economy of eliminating the third and fourth years and continuing many church-related institutions as junior colleges.

The creation of the first junior colleges of this type probably antedated by a few years the creation of junior colleges as an upward extension of high schools. Both types of junior college, however, grew materially in number during the first two decades of the twentieth century. Although the practice of transforming church-related four-year colleges into junior colleges was fairly widespread in the states east of the Rocky Mountains, the largest number of such junior colleges are found in the southern and southeastern United States.

Education opportunities for rural areas. Three states—Mississippi, New York, and Oklahoma—have a number of junior colleges which evolved totally, or in part from efforts at the state level to improve the educational opportunities of boys and girls living in small towns or rural areas. A fourth state, Arkansas, was also in this category at one time, but has since transformed all such institutions into four-year colleges.

Although the principle underlying the creation of the forerunners of these junior colleges was virtually the same in the three states— i.e., to provide enhanced educational opportunities for young people living in small towns or rural areas—the methods of establishing the original educational institutions varied widely.

The forerunner of most of the public junior colleges in the state of Mississippi was the agricultural high school. In the days before the advent of good roads and automobiles, when many rural families were in a very real sense isolated, the establishment by the state of such agricultural high schools in rural areas brought educational opportunities to young people that would otherwise have been denied them. Isolation yielded eventually to the coming of better roads, better means of transportation, and school consolidation. When this happened, the need for the agricultural high schools disappeared. But, instead of being discontinued, the schools were transformed into junior colleges. Thus, the majority of the public junior colleges in Mississippi today owe their origin to the agricultural high school.

The Agricultural and Technical Institutes of New York State originated in small population centers and provided vocational education for terminal students. Carefully avoiding the title *junior college,* these technical institutes offered no courses which would provide transfer credits to four-year colleges. In time, through state-imposed regulations, these institutes were required to add a general education program to their curriculums. Subsequently, they added college-transfer programs, and are now correctly classifiable as junior colleges. Although they comprise a minority of all the junior colleges, public and private, in the state, their existence was definitely an influencing factor in the expansion of the junior colleges in New York.

The first legislature of the State of Oklahoma established six secondary agricultural schools in 1908. Three of these currently exist as junior colleges: Cameron State Agricultural College, Connors State Agricultural College, and Murray State Agricultural College. These junior colleges have exercised a significant influence on the development of such educational institutions in the state.

Other junior colleges have been established in Oklahoma. Some of them are under state auspices; others represent the upward extension of high schools; still others are under private control. All, however, have been influenced in their development by the junior colleges which were the outgrowth of the agricultural high schools.

The creation of junior colleges. Many junior colleges came into existence *as* junior colleges, and were established by individuals or groups motivated by philanthropic desires. These junior colleges, generally referred to as the *independents,* have self-perpetuating boards and are found throughout the country. The greatest concentration of them, however, is in the northeastern section of the country.

The category of independent junior colleges includes some institutions which originated as proprietary schools, founded as profit-making enterprises. Many were family-owned, some were the property of larger groups of stockholders. Regional accrediting organizations in general, however, did not look with favor on the proprietary junior college's application for accreditation. This policy, in many cases, led such colleges to surrender their original charters and apply for new charters as nonprofit organizations. Today, the proprietary junior college has all but disappeared.

Public and Private Junior Colleges

Thus far, major consideration has been given to four types of junior colleges. A fifth type, the proprietary, received some attention in the discussion of independent junior colleges. It is desirable, however, to define the two major categories under which these types may be subsumed. These major categories are *the public* and *the private*.

The distinction between public and private junior colleges is identical with that which obtains between public and private four-year colleges, universities, secondary schools, or elementary schools. Public educational institutions are controlled by boards, the members of which are either elected by the citizens or appointed by publicly elected officials. They are supported mainly from public funds derived from tax sources. Although the patterns of control and support vary, they remain constant in the definition of public junior colleges.

Private junior colleges, by contrast, are controlled by boards whose members are selected by some nongovernmental agency, or by members of the board itself. The support of private junior colleges comes largely from nongovernmental sources: endowments, gifts, grants from private organizations, and tuition fees.

The distinctions between public and private junior colleges have many exceptions. Some public junior colleges have substantial endowments from which income is derived, and many receive gifts from nonpublic sources. Some private institutions receive grants from the federal government, and nearly all enjoy a very real income in the form of exemption from property taxes. Furthermore, many public junior colleges charge fees for tuition. For these reasons, the distinction between public and private junior colleges cannot be sharply drawn on the basis of their sources of financial support. The sharpest differentiation is on the basis of control.

In recent years the term *community college* has come to be widely used as a designation for some junior colleges. There is no formal definition commonly accepted for the community college, but the term is generally used to designate a junior college that is under local public control, and that has a program especially geared to the needs of the community in which it is located. Throughout this treatise, the older and more comprehensive term, *junior college*, will be used, and the kind of institution now frequently called *community college* will be referred to as *local public junior college*. It may be noted, in passing, that in the community in which a junior college is located, the school is commonly referred to as *the college*, without the qualifying *junior;* this is particularly true in communities which have no other institution of higher education.

Variations.   Another situation that should be noted in considering the growth of junior colleges in the United States is the wide variation in the types of institutions that have been classified under this designation. For a time, the four-year junior college, comprising Grades 11–14, was fairly popular. Privately controlled commercial colleges generally did not require a high school diploma for admission and yet, in at least one state, they were considered junior colleges. The institutions called *county teachers colleges,* found in Wisconsin, were—for a few years—classified as junior colleges by the *Junior College Directory*, published annually by the American Association of Junior Colleges; in the recent published volume, *American Junior Colleges*, these county teachers colleges are not included. In some states university extension centers are classified as junior colleges; in others they are not. Frequently, there is disagreement over the classification of institutions by the U.S. Office of Education and the American Association of Junior Colleges.

Junior colleges, as the examples given illustrate, are not easy to define. For this reason, data concerning the number and type of junior colleges, must be accepted with many reservations. At best, the data quoted in this publication and elsewhere can serve only to give a general picture. Their accuracy cannot be accepted without some reservations. The data used in this chapter are taken from *Junior College Directory, 1963.*[1]

Patterns of distribution.   In the academic year, 1900–1901,

---

[1] Edmund J. Gleazer, Jr., *Junior College Directory, 1963* (Washington, D.C.: American Association of Junior Colleges, 1964).

there were eight junior colleges in the United States, each of which had about one hundred students. All were privately supported and controlled. By 1915–16, the total number of junior colleges had increased to 74, with 55 private and 19 public institutions. Total enrollments in the two types were 1771 and 592, respectively—a total of 2363 students.

By 1921–22, the enrollment in the public junior colleges exceeded that in the private institutions (8349 to 7682) although the number of private junior colleges was greater (137 to 70). Private junior colleges continued to outnumber the public institutions until after World War II. By 1947–48, the number was approximately equal: 328 public schools and 323 private ones. In 1959–60, however, the number of public colleges was substantially greater than the private (390 to 273).

The advantage in the number of students enrolled in public junior colleges, first noted in 1921–22, grew progressively more pronounced. In 1938–39, just before the outbreak of World War II, there were approximately 197,000 students enrolled in public junior colleges as compared with 140,500 enrolled in private schools. By 1959–60, 712,000 students—or over 87 per cent of the junior college students in this country—were enrolled in public junior colleges; 104,000 were in the private institutions.

Despite the fact that public junior colleges have outnumbered the private schools for almost twenty years, and have exceeded their enrollment for over forty years, it would be a mistake to conclude that the private junior colleges are on the way out. Both types are growing in number and in enrollment.

The preceding analysis provides one basis for observing the growth of junior colleges in the United States: the number of institutions and the number of students enrolled. Their growth may be observed in another dimension: the spread of junior colleges through the several states. (The data cited, like those given earlier, are derived from *Junior College Directory*,[2] but are based on a different set of statistics.)

In 1919, there were in existence approximately one hundred of the junior colleges that are in operation today. Of this number, 64—or approximately two thirds, were in ten states. The states,

[2] *Ibid.*

with one exception, were located in three geographical areas: the West Coast (California); the Midwest (Illinois, Kansas, Minnesota, and Missouri); and the East Coast (Massachusetts, New York, North Carolina, and Virginia). The single exception was Texas.

During that year, there were sixteen states with no junior colleges, and fifteen with only one junior college each. The other states had either two or three junior colleges each.

Ten years later, in 1929, junior colleges had spread over almost all of the country, with the exception of the Rocky Mountain states and the northwest. In 1919, there were only ten states with four or more junior colleges; by 1929, this number had increased to twenty-three. In 1929, the number of states with only one junior college had dropped to eight, and the number without any had dropped to nine.

By 1939, states in all geographical areas had junior colleges; thirty states had four or more; only five states had just one each; only six had none. In 1949, the number of states with four or more junior colleges had increased to thirty-four; the number with only one had dropped to four, which is what it was in 1964; and the number without any was down to three. In 1959, there were thirty-eight states with four or more junior colleges; only one (Nevada) without any.

Summary

Junior colleges increased from eight in 1900–1901, with an enrollment of one hundred students, to 663 in 1959–60, with an enrollment of 816,000 students. Public junior colleges have increased in number and enrollment much more rapidly than private junior colleges. It has been noted, however, that although the private junior colleges are much smaller from the standpoint of enrollment, they still occupy a significant position in the field. In 1919, only ten states had as many as four or more junior colleges; forty years later, this number had increased to thirty-eight. In 1919, there were sixteen states with no junior colleges and fifteen with only one; forty years later, only one state had no junior college; only four states had just one junior college. In 1919, the states with junior colleges were located in only four geographical areas. In 1964, junior colleges were found in every geographical section of the continental United States, and also in Alaska, Hawaii, the Canal Zone, Puerto Rico, and the Virgin Islands.

This summary gives some idea of the rapid growth and spread of junior colleges in this country. It is on the basis of this background that these educational institutions will now be examined.

CHAPTER II

Educational Purposes of Junior Colleges

The institutional purposes claimed by schools and colleges provide an index to the nature of their educational programs. The validity of this principle may be observed in the fact that regional accrediting associations use such statements of purpose as the starting point in assessing the application of a college for accreditation. In following such a procedure, however, the representatives of the regional accrediting association demand evidence that the college is fulfilling its stated purposes, that its facilities are adequate to these purposes, and that these purposes will be fulfilled in the future.

In this chapter, the stated goals of the junior college will be used as a means for describing its program. No effort will be expended to present substantiating evidence of attainment of the purposes.

Not all the purposes listed are necessarily claimed by the junior college itself. Many represent claims made by proponents of junior colleges who have no direct connection with the institutions. They are, in essence, proposals of goals which should be served by a junior college. No attempt will be made to distinguish between the two sources.

Categories of Purpose

One of the best treatments of the stated purposes of junior colleges is the two-volume publication, *The Junior College*, by L. V. Koos.[1] The author, under a grant from the Commonwealth Fund, made an exhaustive study of all aspects of the junior colleges—both from direct observation and from a thorough study of the literature on the subject. The validity of Koos's study is affirmed by the fact that, in the many studies made since his investigation, most of his identified purposes have been cited and comparatively few have been added.

Koos identified twenty-one separate purposes of the junior col-

---

[1] Leonard Vincent Koos, *The Junior College*, Research Publications of the University of Minnesota, Education Series, No. 5 (Minneapolis: University of Minnesota, 1924).

lege, and divided these into five general classifications. The normal development of the junior college during the forty years since Koos's work was published has made six of the purposes he identified of questionable validity. These are not included in the following list. Moreover, because two of the six purposes omitted constituted one of the general classifications, these classifications have been reduced from five to four.

I. *Educational goals*
　　1. To offer two years of work acceptable to colleges and universities.
　　2. To complete the education of terminal students.
　　3. To provide occupational training of junior college grade.
　　4. To popularize higher education.
　　5. To allow for the continuance of home influence during this period of immaturity.
　　6. To allow attention to the individual student.
　　7. To offer better opportunities for leadership training.
　　8. To offer better instruction in those school years.
　　9. To allow for exploration.
II. *Organizational goals*
　　10. To foster the evolution of the system of education.
III. *Goals related to the university*
　　11. To relieve the university.
　　12. To making possible the real functioning of the university.
　　13. To assure better preparation for university work.
IV. *Goals related to the community*
　　14. To offer courses designed to meet local needs.
　　15. To alter the cultural tone of the community.

Three additional purposes have been added to this list taken from the study by Koos.[2] From Campbell's study comes the purpose: to provide opportunity for adults; from Medsker's: to provide a program for students with educational deficiencies; and, from Clark: the "open door" policy. Thus, a total of eighteen purposes will be discussed. Campbell's and Medsker's statements appear to fit best under the fourth general classification, and Clark's is most appropriate to the first; they will be considered as parts of these two classifications.

---

[2] Doak S. Campbell, *A Critical Study of the Stated Purposes of the Junior College* (Nashville, Tenn.: George Peabody College for Teachers, 1930); Leland L. Medsker, *The Junior College: Progress and Prospect* (New York: McGraw-Hill Book Company, 1960); and Burton R. Clark, *The Open Door College* (New York: McGraw-Hill Book Company, 1960).

The two years under consideration in the study by Koos are the first and second years of the undergraduate college, sometimes referred to as Grades 13 and 14. The choice of terms used in defining these years is of no significance; for many, however, the distinction is of major importance. For this reason, the reader is invited to select the set of terms he likes best, with complete assurance his choice will not affect the discussion which follows.

Educational goals. The first and second stated purposes are those which are most frequently claimed for the junior college; service to transfer students and to terminal students. There are few junior colleges which do not acknowledge both purposes as valid. In serving the first purpose, the junior college obligates itself to provide an educational program of sufficient comprehensiveness and excellence so that students who plan to transfer to a four-year college will not be penalized. In the second purpose, the junior college, at least in theory, obligates itself to provide a program which will provide a complete course of study for terminal students rather than just two years of a four-year program. The satisfactory completion of this program is usually certified by the Associate in Arts degree. It must not be concluded that terminal students are only those who take vocational courses. Many junior college curriculums contain a general education program for terminal students.

The third stated purpose, the provision of occupational training of junior college grade, has particular pertinence to one of the sociotechnological changes listed in Chapter I. It was pointed out there that the rapid technological progress made since the end of World War II has created a whole new category of occupations generally subsumed under the generic title, *technicians.* It was further pointed out that qualification for such occupations required a prolonged period of training—a period longer than that afforded during the high school years. Such training also typically requires greater maturity than is characteristic of high school students.

The provision of occupational training of junior college grade raises a controversial question concerning the nature of the occupations for which training should be provided. The dispute probably will never be resolved. The student of the junior college, however, should be aware of the controversy. To some, *of junior college grade* means any occupation for which up to two years post-high school training is required. Others maintain that *of junior col-*

lege grade refers merely to the junior college as an agency serving the community and that, as such, it should provide occupational training for any type of job whether or not the training is of post-high school level.

The fourth purpose is to popularize higher education. The validity of this purpose is less evident now than it was when identified by Koos in 1920. At that time, the popular demand for higher education was far less pronounced than it is at present. It was pointed out in Chapter I that the current popularity of higher education is the result of the influence of three factors, and none of these factors was operative in 1920. The principle involved in this purpose, however, is well established. Its influencing force, although seriously curtailed, is nonetheless effective. The principle, in brief, is that the location of a collegiate institution near the residences of its potential students invariably increases the enrollment in the college. Proximity definitely exercises an attracting force.

The fifth purpose ascribed to the junior college is the making possible of a continuing home influence for young people during immaturity. It should be acknowledged that this purpose often proves far more acceptable to parents than to potential students. As a matter of fact, some studies of young people's attitudes toward attending local institutions reveals a negative slant, growing out of a desire to be away from home. Regardless of the attitudes of parents or of young people, however, a local junior college does make possible a continuing home influence for those boys and girls who are immature.

There are two related purposes, not identified in the preceding list, which nevertheless deserve consideration. These are: (1) to make it possible for junior college students to hold part-time jobs in their home community to help defray college expenses, and (2) to afford many students who could not afford a four-year college education away from home a less expensive two years at home on which to build the four-year program.

In some public junior colleges, the operation of the first of these principles frequently involves so many students that the academic day is interrupted at 1:00 P.M. and resumed in the evening. Many of the students work at part-time jobs during the interval and return for the evening session.

Another fairly popular variant of this program is the uninterrupted schedule, starting in the morning and running until around 10:00 P.M. or later. Under this arrangement faculty members and students usually have their schedules worked out so as to require their attendance in either the morning or the afternoon.

The opportunity which the junior college provides for a less expensive first two years of undergraduate education has led some to refer to this institution as *the poor man's college*. The economies junior college students enjoy are mainly in the form of less expensive room and board (from living at home) and lower transportation costs involved in getting to and from school.

The sixth purpose, that of affording attention to the individual student, is probably much less valid currently than at the time it was identified by Koos. It rested on the principle that junior colleges typically had small enrollments and small classes, permitting close attention to be given to individual students. In 1921–22, there were 16,031 students enrolled in 207 junior colleges—an average of approximately seventy-seven students per college. In 1959–60, 510,642 students (exclusive of adult and special students) were enrolled in 663 junior colleges—an average of 770 per college. Thus, in a period of approximately forty years, the number of junior colleges has increased only 3.2 times, but the number of students per college has increased tenfold. There is no doubt that attention is given to individual students in some junior colleges, but the opportunities for doing so are decreasing.

The seventh purpose—to provide a better opportunity for leadership training—rests on the same principle as that underlying the purpose just discussed. A student in a junior college with a small enrollment has a better chance of developing leadership traits than one in a school with a larger student body. For this reason, increases in enrollment decrease the opportunities for attaining this purpose.

The next purpose listed involves offering better instruction in these school years. It should be observed that the validity of this purpose rests far more on the logic of the situation than it does on empirical evidence. The logic advanced to support this claim is that the teaching staff of the junior college can devote all their time to their instructional responsibilities, because they are not obligated to participate in research activities. Furthermore, it is pointed out that many junior college teachers are recruited directly from secondary schools, where their entire orientation was in the direction of excellence in teaching. The third part of the logic draws attention to the fact that in many four-year colleges, particularly those associated with graduate schools, much of the instruction at the freshman and sophomore levels is delegated to graduate students. The argument does not disparage the competence of such students to provide excellent teaching in the classroom; rather, it suggests that the loyalties of such students are divided between teaching and completing a graduate program and also that, as a result of their status, they have less time to devote to being good teachers.

There is one item related to this claimed purpose. The junior college is less likely to impose high admission standards than are many four-year colleges and universities. The net result is that there is a greater likelihood that junior college classes will contain a wide range of student ability. To the extent that this greater heterogeneity prevails in junior college classrooms, there is a demand for more efficient instruction there than elsewhere.

The claimed purpose of allowing for exploration, contrary to the sixth and seventh purposes, is probably more valid currently than it was at the time it was first identified. This probability is attested by two developments which have occurred in the forty-year span.

The first of these developments is the increased proportion of college-age people who are actually attending college. As this proportion continues to increase, which appears to be likely, the number of boys and girls who go into full-time employment at or before the time of high school graduation will decrease correspondingly. This can only mean that for an increasing number of young people job-selection decisions will be postponed and, as a consequence, there will be additional time for thinking about them.

The second development comprises changes in the nature of preparation programs required for entrance into managerial or professional occupations. There changes have resulted in a postponement, by one or two years, of the specialized courses included in these programs. Examples of these changes may be seen in three fields: engineering, teaching, and medicine.

At the time that this claimed purpose was identified, the first year of the engineering curriculum was devoted to general engineering. Specialized courses began in the sophomore year. Not only has specialization been postponed but the program of the first year or two has a greater portion of general education courses in addition to the traditional general engineering.

Forty years ago, teaching certificates in many states were issued on the basis of two years of college work, and—in some instances—even less. Now the specialized courses in pedagogy, once taken in the freshman and sophomore years, have been postponed to the third, fourth, or even the fifth year. The first two years are now customarily devoted to a solid program in general education as a basis for professional education.

Preparation for entrance into medical schools has also changed. Forty years ago, the student who aspired to enter medical school took two years of highly specialized courses. Today, the period of premedical study has been lengthened to four years, and the number of required courses has been reduced.

The effect of these two developments—the progressive increase in the proportion of college-age young people in college whose vocational decisions are thereby postponed, and the greater latitude for course selection in the freshman and sophomore years caused by the postponement of required and specialized courses to the third, fourth, or even the fifth year—is to give greater validity to the junior college's goal of allowing for exploration.

The tenth of the claimed purposes of the junior college is to provide an opportunity for adult education. (This purpose, it will be recalled was taken from Campbell's list.) The story of the development of adult education in the United States would require far more space than exists in this monograph. What is of significance here is the role of the junior colleges in this great movement.

Data for 1959–60 show that approximately 51 per cent of all junior colleges in the United States provide programs for adult students. Since comparatively few private junior colleges include such programs, the percentage of public junior colleges providing such education would be substantially higher. Enrollments in excess of 130,000 are reported. These data indicate that the junior college's claim of providing educational programs for adults is substantiated.

The last of the claimed purposes under the first general classification is the one taken from Medsker's study, that of providing a program for students with educational deficiencies. Although the implications of this claimed purpose are numerous, three have been selected to illustrate its operation.

The first of these concerns the so-called remedial programs included in the educational programs of many junior colleges. Two of the fields in which such programs are needed are communication and mathematics. Many students are graduated from high schools deficient in reading skills, in oral and written expression, and in basic mathematical skills. Noncredit remedial courses often enable students to overcome these weaknesses and thus successfully to complete college careers.

A second example concerns students who have had unsuccessful records in four-year colleges. "Salvage" operations have been performed successfully by junior colleges, and students who would otherwise have dropped out of college permanently are given a second chance.

The third implication of this purpose is related directly to the raising of admission standards by four-year colleges. It was pointed out in Chapter I that this device is being used by many colleges and universities to limit enrollment. As admission standards are raised, more and more high school graduates are unable to meet them. In many instances, though not all by any means, these deficiencies can be overcome through a satisfactory academic record compiled in an accredited junior college. At the end of two years, the student with a successful record can qualify for entrance into the junior year of the college or university for which his high school record was inadequate to qualify him for admission as a freshman.

Organizational goals. The second general classification concerns the organizational goals of junior colleges. It includes a major purpose: to foster the evolution of the system of education.

Although the American ideal has long been twelve years of free public education, a serious attempt to attain it has been made only within comparatively recent times. Each successive year, a higher and higher percentage of secondary school students are remaining in school. Although the percentage figures indicate that a material amount of progress must be made before the ideal can be said to be fairly well achieved, the progress that has been made to date has led to public advocacy of the extension of free public education to what is regarded by some as its logical limit—the extension upward from the twelfth to the fourteenth year.

One of the most influential publications dealing with this topic was issued in 1964 by the Educational Policies Commission under the title of *Universal Opportunity for Education Beyond the High School*. The main theme of this book is that free public education should be provided for all the young people of this country through the fourteenth year. The favorable reception received from a wide range of individuals and organizations indicates the idea has much popular support.

The ideal involved in the purpose of fostering the evolution of the system of education, however, involves more than the mere upward extension of high schools through the first two years of college. It means a reconsideration of the concept of secondary education.

From the standpoint of the scope of education provided, college students in the 1960's acquire, by the end of the sophomore year, the equivalent of what college students in 1800 received by the end of the senior year. Thus, from a functional viewpoint, it is correct to refer to the junior college as, simply, a college. Moreover, if the baccalaureate degree signifies the completion of college work, it was the critics of the University of Chicago, and not the University, who were out of step in criticizing the University for awarding the baccalaureate degree at the end of what would be normally regarded as the sophomore year.

Unfortunately, stereotypes concerning the organization of education in the United States are built on chronological spans rather than functions. The college, for example, ends with the sixteenth year, not the fourteenth, although the thirteenth and fourteenth years are often more similar to the eleventh and twelfth than to the fifteenth and sixteenth. Another example of a stereotype is the term *high school,* with its concluding year the twelfth. The force of such stereotypes is so great that it usually closes the minds of thinking people to any arguments which violate them.

Functionally, secondary education in practice provides two achievements for the student who completes it. He has rounded out a minimum program of general education, and he has either completed the basic preparation for advanced specialization in an academic or professional field, or has acquired sufficient vocational education to warrant his entry full-time in employment. For many students, neither of the two options under the second achievement is reached. Instead, these students take additional general education courses.

The satisfactory discharge of the function of secondary education requires two years beyond graduation from high school. Thus, the fostering of the evolution of the system of education involves the extension of the program of secondary education through the fourteenth year.

Cognizance has already been taken of the fact that there is strong opposition to this development. An interesting commentary on this opposition is that much of it stems from junior college leaders. It is probable that in most instances they are thinking along the lines dictated by the previously described stereotype. *Secondary education* means *high school education,* and junior colleges are not high schools or extensions of them but, in their judgment, an inextricable part of higher education.

This case of opposition from junior college leaders raises a question as to the validity of the claimed purpose. It is probable, however, that what currently appears to be an impasse—evolution of a system checked by the opposition of a group who are directly concerned with its implications—may resolve itself through the development of state systems of junior colleges with the control located in the board of the district junior college. The only step not now taken, but essential to the evolutionary concept, would be the development of greater liaison between the high schools and the junior colleges—liaison in such areas as cooperative curriculum planning.

Goals related to the university. The third general classification of claimed purposes for junior colleges includes those affecting the university. The first purpose under this classification is "to relieve the university." Again, the validity of this purpose has changed since the time it was first identified. In this instance, the validity has become increasingly pronounced.

Attention was directed in Chapter I to one of the critical problems now existing in higher education: the accommodation of record-breaking demands for admission to institutions of higher education. It was pointed out in that chapter that, in many of the plans being devised to solve this problem, more and more consideration is being given to junior colleges.

The obvious relief which junior colleges can provide to universities in this situation needs no elaboration. Some further understanding of the value of this service may be facilitated through a brief look at two illustrations.

For many years, the Engineering College of the University of California has relied on the junior colleges in that state to help carry the load of freshman and sophomore engineering students. The liaison developed between these two groups has assured the students' smooth transition from the second year of the junior college to the third year of the Engineering College. Also, junior colleges have been given some freedom to develop innovational arrangements of the curriculum—always acting within the framework of purposes of the Engineering College. Thus, the junior colleges not only cooperate in carrying the load of freshman and sophomores, but also cooperate in the work of curriculum development.

The second illustration of junior colleges relieving the university is found in the state of Florida. Florida Atlantic University, which was founded in 1964, has dispensed with the freshman and sophomore years altogether: entering students enroll in the junior year. This arrangement is in line with state planning, which recently brought a large number of junior colleges into existence.

The second claimed purpose of junior colleges under the general classification of university relations is "to make possible the real functioning of the university." This purpose, in a very real sense, is the opposite side of the coin that dealt with the evolution of the school system. The emphasis here is on assuming the functions of the first two years of the undergraduate college, previously described in this report as the culminating years of secondary education. This leaves the university free to concentrate its staff, resources, and energies on a genuine program of higher—i.e., specialized—education.

The concept of higher education considered in the preceding paragraph is not a new one. More than a century ago, Tappan at the University of Michigan, and Folwell at the University of Minnesota, were advocating the removal of the first two years from the university campus. Their pleas may be summarized in very few words. The freshman and sophomore years serve merely to complete the student's preparation for entrance into the realm of higher education. Since a university is concerned primarily with higher education, it should not have to dissipate its resources in order to do for students what should have been done before they arrived at the university. This preparation should be a prerequisite for university entrance.

The third purpose under the general classification considered reads, "to assure better preparation for university work." Koos, in commenting on this purpose which he identified, says,

> Those who propose . . . [it] look to see *an improvement in the preparation of students for university work,* but they fail to mention the grounds for their hopes. These may be implicit in purposes 6 [to afford greater attention to the individual student], 8 [to offer better instruction in those school years] and 9 [to allow for exploration] as already presented.[3]

Goals related to the community. The fourth general classification of claimed purposes of junior colleges involves those affecting the community of location. Three specific purposes may be included under the general heading of community service.

"To offer work designed to meet local needs" is the first of the purposes listed. At the time the purpose was identified, it pertained (according to Koos) to vocational and social needs. In the forty years that have elapsed, a third category of sociological needs has come into existence—the needs of the so-called sick communities.

The reference of Koos to vocational needs in the locality served by the junior college parallels a purpose discussed earlier, that of providing occupational training of junior college grade. The junior college may be expected to provide vocational preparation for the occupations and industries found in its community. His reference to social needs pertains to such areas as the avocational, fine arts, public forums, and such other activities frequently associated with adult evening schools, as well as the regular program.

The area of sociological needs, however, receives far less consideration, although the local junior college is admirably situated to serve these needs through its educational program. The modern community, geographically defined, has a host of sociological problems which will be diminished in part by an educational attack. These problems relate to housing, slums, crime, juvenile delinquency, and many other situations that have become problems through the far-reaching changes that have taken place in the communities in recent years.

---

[3] Leonard V. Koos, *The Junior College Movement* (Boston: Ginn & Company, 1925), p. 26.

Junior colleges bring together, in their instructional and administrative staff, valuable resources in the form of trained personnel. Moreover, the facilities provided in adult evening program seminars, in communitywide studies, and in special short courses dealing with specific aspects of community problems, can do much to bring the best thinking in the community to bear on these problems. It is regrettable that more junior colleges and communities have not found the means to harness these resources and to turn them toward the elimination of the causes for these problems.

The second purpose under the last general classification is "to alter the cultural tone of the community." This purpose connotes a general lifting of the cultural tone of the community. In this sense, it is the same influence that would be exercised by the existence in the community of a four-year college or a university. It stems from the influence that the instructional and administrative staff will exercise as citizens, the contribution made by the physical plant and campus of the junior college, and the assistance derived from its educational program in all its phases.

The last purpose appearing under the general classification of affecting the community of location is that suggested by Clark's book, the operation of an "open door" junior college. The "open door" junior college is just what its name implies—admission doors held wide open to all who wish to enter. To the extent that the principle that any and all education has a positive value can be accepted, the desirability of this purpose is unquestionable. Before a junior college adopts this policy, however, there must be a genuine sympathy for it on the part of all the professional personnel in the college, and there must also be acceptance by the policy-makers of the unmistakable implications of such a policy for a very broad educational program.

This policy can attain optimum success only as the prerequisites described in the preceding paragraph are attained. The heterogeneity of the student body will be far greater in a junior college serving this purpose than in those which do not. Moreover, true satisfaction of the purpose does not imply simply admitting all who apply, and then failing those who are not served by a narrow educational program. The junior college program must be so broadly conceived that it will include elements to serve all who are admitted—an admittedly expensive undertaking in terms of money, staff, resources, and plant.

The attitude of the teaching staff must also be sympathetic with such a policy. The student body can not very well be divided into first-, second-, and third-class citizens. Discrimination against some types of students in certain courses cannot be permitted. The "open door" policy is not intended as an arrangement by which a college for the academically apt takes on an adjunct of miscellaneous individuals who are tolerated for the sake of charity. In maintaining the proper campus spirit, the instructional staff has a tremendous responsibility.

What has been said about the "open door" policy is not intended as negative criticism of the idea; rather, the intent has been to point out that genuine satisfaction of this purpose involves far more than mere public announcement of its existence.

Summary

This completes the list of purposes claimed for junior colleges. Eighteen such purposes are listed and analyzed. The extent of their current validity is commented on in cases in which changes have apparently taken place since the purpose was originally identified.

The reader needs to keep two ideas firmly in mind as a basis for evaluating the purposes of the junior college. First, some of the claimed purposes are made by the staff of the junior colleges themselves through their catalogs; others are made by proponents of junior colleges in the literature dealing with the movement. In the latter category, "purposes" often amount to idealized goals which the junior colleges should undertake to reach. Second, the picture created by the eighteen purposes listed pertain to no individual junior college. They do not constitute eighteen criteria which should be used in evaluating each and every junior college. The only obligations which any individual junior college has is the announcement of its own institutional purposes, and the attempt to live up to them.

The purposes of any junior college conceivably could include all the eighteen purposes listed, but the likelihood is extremely remote. Also, it is conceivable that a junior college might adopt a list of purposes, all valid, none of which appear on this list. This likelihood is equally remote. What is most probable is that any list of institutional purposes announced by an individual junior college would correspond with many—though not all—of those listed in this chapter. The list, taken in the aggregate, portrays only a composite picture of the junior college.

CHAPTER III

The Curriculum of Junior Colleges

The term *curriculum,* as used in professional literature, has many connotations. In order to avoid misunderstanding, it will be used in this chapter to mean *a course of study*—a listing of the several academic and technical fields of study usually found in junior colleges.

The reader will find a close parallel between this chapter on curriculum and Chapter II. This is natural because, if the staff of the junior college is faithful to the announced purposes of the institution, those purposes will be reflected in the curriculum that is developed. This principle is so pronounced in its validity that, when an individual junior college applies for membership in a regional accrediting association, it will be expected to point out at what places in the curriculum may be found the implementation of the purposes.

The discussion of the curriculum in the junior college must be viewed in the same light as that recommended for the purposes: it represents a composite of all junior colleges, and not of any one institution. Junior college curriculums vary widely. Any consideration of the curriculum details of all junior colleges individually would require such a publication as *American Junior Colleges,* in which the section, "Institutional Exhibits," provides a brief description of the curriculum in each of the junior colleges included in the book. The reader should keep this idea constantly in mind if he is not to lose the perspective observed in the writing.

For the sake of convenience, the curriculum has been divided into three major areas: general education, preparatory education (those aspects which prepare the student for specialization in an academic or professional field), and vocational education (those aspects which prepare a student for full-time employment immediately after leaving the junior college).

27

General Education

In the list of purposes considered in the preceding chapter, no specific reference was made to an implied need for general education. This need, however, is implicit in the purpose which advocates fostering evolution of the system of education, and also the purpose which suggests making possible the real functioning of the university. The implication in each of these was that, in many instances, the junior college would enable the student to round out the minimum program of general education he had started in the first grade, and thereby to free him for complete concentration on the specialized program undertaken in the junior year of the undergraduate college.

General education, in this sense, refers to the nonvocational, nonspecialized portion of the student's educational program. This is the portion that applies to his life activities as a citizen, a member of a family, a church-goer, a neighbor. It will include such matters as perfecting effective communication skills, adopting sound principles on personal and public health, developing an appreciation of the fine arts, and developing at least a layman's understanding of the physical environment in which we live.

Students of the field of general education recognize that there are many means by which a general education program may be organized. It may, for example be based on an analysis of the life activities of adults, with the required courses set up on the basis of the major segments of these activities. For many years, Stephens College at Columbia, Missouri, has been the outstanding exponent of this method of organization.[1] This so-called functional organization, however, was never very widespread among the junior colleges.

By far the most popular method of organization of the general education program is based on the accepted academic disciplines. A variant of this which was popular for a time, though less so now, is the survey course—such as a survey of the humanities, of the social sciences, or of the physical sciences. In such courses, a prescribed number of credit hours is usually specified for each of the academic disciplines.

Junior colleges, with few exceptions, have shown little creative-

---

[1] For an interesting account of this program, see Roy Ivan Johnson (ed.), *Explorations in General Education* (New York: Harper & Row, Publishers, 1947).

ness in organizing general education programs. The explanation usually given is that they are bound by the requirements of the four-year colleges to which their students plan to transfer. There was a time when this explanation had far greater validity than it has now. The trend among four-year colleges has been toward a relaxation of such requirements for transfer students. In one state, Florida, the trend has advanced to the point at which a cooperative arrangement has been made among the four-year colleges and the junior colleges which assures that programs of general education developed in the junior colleges and completed by the transfer students will be accepted as satisfying the requirements for general education of the four-year colleges.

Identification of the general education program in the junior college can be made most satisfactorily by examining the list of courses to be completed as a basis for graduation. Required courses usually include English (two years), the social sciences, the natural sciences, mathematics, the humanities, and occasionally the fine arts. Physical education, with a reduced credit value, also appears in most general education programs.

There is a wide diversity among junior colleges as to what proportion of the two-year curriculum students will be required to devote to general education. A rule-of-thumb formula found in many of these institutions is to devote to general education approximately 50 per cent of the total courses required for graduation.

There are several problems associated with the general education program in the junior college. The student should have some familiarity with these problems if he is to avoid uninformed ideas about the subject. A brief consideration will be given to each of the problems. No significance attaches to the order in which these problems are discussed.

Faculty understanding. One problem stems from the failure on the part of many faculty members to achieve an operational understanding of the nature of general education. The causes for this failure vary, making a definitive generalization impossible. In the main, however, it is probable that the greatest barrier to acquiring such an understanding stems from the specialized orientation which graduate preparation in a specific academic field produces in potential faculty members. The physical science instructor, for example, may inveigh against the necessity for requiring separate courses in two or more of the social sciences. He may accept with complete equilibrium the combination of zoology and botany into a general biology course. But he is likely not to understand that his insistence on separate courses in chemistry and physics represents the same principle he opposed in the social sciences, and he is likely to see no virtue whatever in developing a general physical science course for general education purposes along the identical lines that, in the general biology course, brought together zoology and botany.

This problem, stemming in part from the faculty's orientation toward specialization, manifests itself in another way. It has been found that certain courses with traditional titles may be transformed into general education courses if the instructor shifts the emphasis from preparation for advanced-level courses in the same academic field to an emphasis on learning for the sake of immediate, non-technical, nonspecialized use. But to convince an instructor of the desirability of such shift in emphasis, and to get him to make the shift after having acknowledged its desirability, are two very difficult tasks. The habit of viewing all students as potential majors in an academic discipline is a formidable one.

Student motivation.   A second problem confronting the proponents of general education programs is that of student motivation. It must be recalled that the student body in a typical junior college is a highly heterogenous group. Nevertheless, the motivation which leads students to learn definitely includes a desire for specialization. Many of the students—and, in some junior colleges, most of them—have only a vague notion as to their eventual academic or vocational goals, yet learning for the sake of being a better homemaker, a better citizen, or a better member of a neighborhood social group is hardly the motivation they bring with them to the junior college.

In some instances, this lack of a motivating interest in the various aspects of the general education program has led to compromises in junior college policy. Secretarial science presents a good example evolving from this compromise. The traditional secretarial science course in the junior college is typically a two-year program. Part of the course taken is concerned with the technical skills and understandings needed for employment; the rest consists of general education. Most of the students enrolled in such programs are terminal students who plan to go to work immediately after graduation. The motivating interest of such students is strongly vocational.

This attitude frequently makes students resentful of the general education subjects they are required to take. In a sense—a very real sense for them—such courses are a waste of time. They want to get on with the preparation for the jobs they hope to get. Consequently, they may drop out of the program or, more often, accept a position for which they are not fully prepared.

If students follow the second of these procedures, quite often a second pressure may be created on the curriculum-makers of the junior college. Because the students are not fully prepared for the stenographic or clerical jobs they have taken, their work may be below the standards of efficiency the employers demand. As a result, the employers may become adversely critical of the efficiency of the secretarial science program in the junior college.

To offset such pressures, many junior colleges have organized an optional one-year secretarial science program. The traditional two-year program is also retained. The one-year curriculum is most often organized by eliminating the general education requirements of the two-year program. Students who complete the one-year plan obviously do not qualify for the Associate of Arts degree awarded by the junior college. They do, however, reduce the length of their secretarial program by one year, and do go to their employment fully prepared insofar as technical skills and understandings are concerned.

Prescriptions.   Still another problem which has given concern to some curriculum-makers in the junior college grows out of the extent to which the general education program shall be completely prescribed. Shall all students who qualify for graduation be required to complete identical general education programs, or should deviations from these requirements be permitted? The answers to such questions arise from the value systems held by individual faculty members and administrators. In any group of faculty members, these value systems are likely to vary and to produce different answers.

Most junior colleges do have general education programs. They are more frequently identified as requirements for graduation than as general education. Little creativeness may be observed in the construction of most of these programs although the restrictions of transfer requirements are being relaxed. Major problems existing in general education programs in junior colleges are usually the product of lack of faculty understanding or sympathy concerning the concept involved, or of the weak motivational interest of students in mastering the learning required in general education classes.

Preparatory Education

It should be pointed out at the outset that the term *preparatory education* is not generally accepted in the literature. The writer has long used the term, though, and believes it to be the best to convey the meaning intended. Other terms used frequently are *preprofessional,* or *university parallel.* In every instance, however, the term used applies to the courses which students take as a basis for advanced-level specialized courses beyond the junior college in either the academic or professional fields.

The line dividing preparatory courses from general education courses is, at best, a thin one, and in many instances nonexistent. Theoretically, the distinction is found in the purpose to which the education is to be put. In general education, the purpose is immediate, is nontechnical, nonspecialized, nonvocational. In preparatory education, achievement of the purpose is delayed until such time as the student takes the course for which the preparatory education course has qualified him. Some courses are designed to achieve both purposes simultaneously. A course in general inorganic chemistry, for instance, may provide general education for one student and preparation for advanced chemistry courses for another student in the same class.

The difficulties involved in distinguishing between general and preparatory education do not eliminate the desirability of making the distinction. The claimed purposes of junior colleges explicitly or implicitly stress the need for each type. Moreover, the distinction simplifies the work of those staff members responsible for developing the curriculum of the junior college. The separation of these two major areas of the curriculum permits more detailed attention to be given to the planning.

Transfer value. The preparatory segment of the junior college curriculum is under constant evaluation because upon its quality depends the success of transfer students in advanced courses at a four-year college or university. This constant pressure leads many junior college staffs to give more attention to this aspect of the curriculum than to any other part. It is a highly vulnerable part of the curriculum and any carelessness in course development becomes apparent rapidly.

It is in this particular aspect of the program that a major problem is encountered. Attention to maintenance of high standards in preparatory courses usually takes the form of frequent checks with the four-year colleges to which the junior college students transfer, to keep pace with changes in course content, prerequisites, or credit-hour values of courses. The problem arises when it is discovered that the colleges to which the students transfer differ in regard to course content, prerequisites, and credit-hour values. The curriculum-planner for the junior college, as a consequence of this lack of uniformity, must become an academic juggler, keeping as many "balls" in the air as there are colleges to which the students will transfer.

This problem, fortunately, is not as serious as it once was. Four-year colleges are relaxing some of the rigidity of the transfer requirements, are becoming more disposed to accept equivalent courses as substitutes for specified courses, and are progressively moving more and more specialized courses out of the freshman and sophomore years. As these developments occur, the planning of the preparatory program in the junior college becomes easier.

Ease of establishment.   Despite the problem of gearing the junior college preparatory program to the requirements of four-year colleges, this program remains the heart of most junior college curriculums. There are probably several reasons for this. One of the most prominent of these probable reasons may be observed in the relative ease with which these programs may be set up.

In the first place, needed instructors for such programs are easier to locate than, for example, instructors for the upper division of four-year colleges, or instructors for the vocational department of the junior college. By far the greatest proportion of instructors in junior colleges have a master's degree, with—at most—some graduate work beyond it. This means that those who employ faculty members for junior colleges are not in the more competitive market for individuals with doctorates.

Junior college instructors in vocational departments most often are expected to have both a master's degree and successful trade or technical experience. This combination is in short supply, and in many instances, the lack of college preparation has to be remedied by substituting a number of years of practical experience for a certain amount of formal preparation.

The relative ease of setting up a preparatory program is probably accounted for also by the ready availability of classroom facilities. It should be kept in mind that this program in the junior college concerns only the freshman and sophomore levels. Courses at this level do not require the specialized facilities demanded by advanced-level courses.

Added to the factor of availability is the lower cost of these facilities. The college level served by the preparatory program eliminates the much greater cost of the more specialized facilities required at advanced levels.

Not only are the facilities needed for the preparatory program available and comparatively inexpensive, but the expansion of the junior college program is also comparatively inexpensive. A junior college offering only a first-year program in mathematics faces no staggering cost if it adds a second year. Moreover, a junior college offering only history courses in the first two years can spread its program to include government, or some of the other social sciences, without a tremendous expansion of the budget. Thus, the third probable cause for the popularity of the preparatory programs will be found in the fact that they are comparatively inexpensive to expand either upward or outward.

The fourth probable cause for the popularity of preparatory programs is related to the generally recognized popularity of the professions as vocational goals. The point has already been made on two occasions that the trend in professional education, especially those professions entry into which is based on either a baccalaureate or a master's degree, is to locate the more specialized courses into the third, fourth, or fifth years. This leaves the first two years free for liberal arts courses. On this basis, a fairly small complement of such liberal arts courses will satisfy the preprofessional requirements for several professions. Koos pointed this situation out in the study alluded to earlier. His observations have become even more valid as a result of the trend described above.

A fifth probable cause underlying the comparative ease of organizing a program in preparatory education lies in the fact that these programs can be offered by junior colleges with small enrollments. The point was made in Chapter II that many junior colleges are growing larger. Still, it must be kept in mind that there are— and probably will always be—many junior colleges with small enrollments. *Junior College Directory, 1963* reports 196, or slightly over 30 per cent of all the junior colleges accounted for, had enrollments of 199 or fewer students. Although there is no consensus as to what level of enrollment serves as the dividing line between junior colleges that are "small" and those that are not, most observers would agree all 199 educational institutions should be classified as small. Thus, the popularity of the preparatory program in small junior colleges is a matter of significance.

The sixth probable cause for the situation under consideration relates to the popularity of such preparatory programs with the regional accrediting associations. Successive revisions of accrediting standards for junior colleges have made these standards more comprehensive in regard to the total junior college program. Nevertheless, preparatory programs still occupy a prominent place in these standards, as will be attested to by junior college administrators who have served as hosts to the representatives of the accrediting associations.

The seventh probable cause, then, is that a junior college with a strong preparatory program comes nearer to the popular image of what a college should be. The favorable impression allegedly made by a preparatory program would produce popular support for it and lead to greater public sympathy for the junior college. The probable validity of the seventh cause for the ease with which the preparatory program can be organized is more conjectural than any of the preceding six.

What, then, is preparatory education? One definition has already been supplied: it is the program which prepares a student for advanced-level specialization in the academic and the professional fields. Defined operationally, it comprises the courses which are popularly called *the liberal arts.*

Vocational Education

The vocational segment of the junior college curriculum is responsible for imparting skills and understandings necessary for the student who plans to enter full-time employment after leaving the junior college. In this sense, it serves primarily the terminal student, the one who has no intention of transferring to the junior year of a four-year college.

Vocational programs are not nearly so widespread among junior colleges as are the other areas of the curriculum previously considered. Almost every junior college has a general education program, and a preponderant majority have preparatory programs, but vocational programs are found in only two thirds of the institutions.[2] If the junior colleges with only one or two vocational fields are not considered, the figure would drop to less than one half.

Types.   The various aspects of business account for the greatest number of vocational courses in the junior colleges. Of these, secretarial and clerical courses are by far the most popular. This is accounted for not only by the universal demand for stenographic and clerical workers, but also by the fact that these are the only two fields in which the private junior colleges offer programs with any frequency.

One significant development in the vocational programs of junior colleges is the substantial increase of programs classifiable as engineering technology, and the corresponding decrease in those fields commonly found under the classification of trade and industrial. The latter category, in the main, comprises those vocational areas of skilled trades found also in secondary school programs. The former category is representative of the emerging occupations subsumed under the general heading of "technicians." Although the greatest number of programs offered by the junior colleges involves trades and industrial occupations, the technician programs have made substantial gains.

Another field which is showing increased popularity among junior colleges is nursing. This field includes programs leading to the

---

[2] Support for this statement is found in the listing of vocational programs in Edmund J. Gleazer, Jr. (ed.), *American Junior Colleges,* 6th ed. (Washington, D.C.: American Council on Education, 1964). Subsequent statements about the incidence of vocational programs are taken from the same source.

certificate of Licensed Registered Nurse and those leading to the certificate of Licensed Vocational Nurse.

Altogether, a total of 95 different vocational programs are offered by the junior colleges in the United States, ranging from agriculture to X-ray technology, and representing a wide spread of occupational titles. They also indicate considerable ingenuity on the part of those who plan the programs in finding new occupational fields for which the need for vocational training exists.

At this point in the discussion of vocational education, it is appropriate to comment on the situation prevailing in junior colleges with a broad vocational program—a situation which makes of these junior colleges, in essence, dual-curriculum institutions. The separateness of the two parts of the organization is caused by some basic differences in the curriculums, the purposes of the students, the faculty, and the nature of instruction.

The academic curriculum of the junior college is dictated largely by the logic of the academic disciplines represented. The courses selected are those which will fit best into the four-year program leading to the baccalaureate degree. The institution's goal is realized when students taking these academic courses can get full credit for them upon transfer to four-year colleges.

The vocational curriculum of the junior college is controlled by the types of skills and understandings required for successful entrance into full-time employment in given occupational fields. The selection of courses is consistent with principles of efficiency in organizing education for occupational competence. The specific occupational field, not the next higher level of college education, is the dominant force. The courses taken are often nontransferable and are so labeled in the catalog.

Students and faculty. Students enrolled in the academic curriculum purport to be preparing for the third year of the undergraduate program. The reservation implied in the use of the term *purport* acknowledges that many students enrolled in this curriculum never reach the third year because they drop out after or even before graduation from the junior college.

The vocational students are terminal students. Their attention is centered on the occupation for which they are preparing and which they will enter upon graduation. As was indicated above, they frequently resent required courses for which they see no need.

The formal preparation of the four-year college preparatory faculty is academic. Their language is academic. Their professional pride is most frequently manifested by membership in a professional academic organization and in subscriptions to professional periodicals.

Vocational teachers, on the other hand, are more often products of professional schools than of colleges of liberal arts. Whether graduates of such schools or not, they have a background of experience as active practitioners in the occupational field for which they are providing occupational training or in a related field. Their professional affiliations and reading material are selected on the same basis as those of the academic teachers—the field of their greatest interest.

Academic instruction is largely aimed at developing mental processes. Very few manual skills are included, except perhaps for skills in laboratory techniques. Academic learning is verbal learning; the concern is for progress in the "pure," the basic disciplines. The library is an essential part of academic life.

It would be an inexcusable mistake to infer from this that vocational education does not concern itself with mental processes. The difference between vocational instruction and academic learning— as far as mental processes are concerned—is one of degree. Vocational instruction in the junior college emphasizes development of skills rather than the mental processes. The typist who could give a scholarly treatise on the social implications of the typewriter, but could type only fifteen words per minute, would hardly be suited to a stenographic job. Vocational instruction is concerned with the applied, the professional disciplines. The shop is an essential part of the vocational program.

Organization. This dual nature of many junior colleges has been the subject of some interesting developments. One of these is the suggestion that the junior college give up its preparatory program and devote all its energy to providing for terminal students. This move died out when it became apparent that all the resources of higher education would be needed to accommodate the great numbers who were seeking admission to colleges and universities.

The vocational aspect of the dual program has frequently been criticized by those who regard a college education as inconsistent with programs to train technicians and stenographers. Basing their attack on the traditional liberal arts curriculum, these critics have seriously questioned the admission of junior colleges to respectable academic circles. But they have only displayed their own lack of information when they described junior college transfer students in four-year colleges as "distinctly inferior": the charge is clearly refuted by the facts.

Other ramifications of the dual nature of junior colleges exist. A significant fact is often overlooked: a dual-curriculum educational institution can exist without internal strife, and can continually provide a highly proficient program for both groups of students.

Vocational education programs in junior colleges are usually organized in one or more of some four general ways. All four methods may be used in various parts of the total program within a given junior college.

One method is that used in the organization of any other two-year curriculum. Vocational courses are set up with lecture and shops, and prerequisite courses are taken in a given order. In addition to the vocational or technical part of his schedule, the student will take certain courses in general education. By combining these two parts of the program, the student will qualify at the end of the two years for the associate degree.

A second method of organization is generally referred to as *the cooperative plan*. The distinctive feature of this plan is that the student's schedule calls for his spending part of the time in classes, and part of the time on a job in the occupational field for which he is preparing or in a closely related field. The on-the-job part of his schedule includes planned instructional experiences. Several methods have been employed in scheduling the in-class, on-the-job division of the student's time. One of the more popular of the arrangements is for the student to be half the day in classes and the other half on the job. Another arrangement is that of pairing students at registration. Following this method, one student will be on the job while the other attends classes. At the end of the specified time, the two students change places. This system continues until the students have completed their programs.

A third method of organization was described earlier in this chapter in connection with programs in secretarial science. In this method, the length of the program is curtailed by eliminating all general education courses. Thus, the student is able to complete the vocational training in a shorter time, but forfeits any chance of a degree.

The fourth method of organizing vocational programs is on the basis of short-unit courses. No attempt is made to provide for a comprehensive occupational program. Segments are selected, such as aspects of welding or repair of farm machinery. These programs may be organized for intensive work over a short period of time or may be spaced over a longer period of time.

Another aspect of the organization of vocational education programs in junior colleges is the frequent use of lay advisory committees. These committees are composed of people engaged in occupations identical with, or closely related to, those for which the junior colleges is providing training. They usually serve as advisers to teachers or departments. Frequent conferences are held by the instructors and their respective advisory committees to discuss such subjects as newly developed processes or equipment, specific skills and understandings needed on the job, and more efficient ways of training students. The instructor brings to the conference his technical skill in the occupation and his professional competence as a teacher. The committee member brings his competence as an employee or worker and his first-hand knowledge of the latest developments in the field.

It was pointed out earlier that vocational programs of any magnitude at all are found in less than half the junior colleges in the country. Since the programs have proved their worth in the junior colleges in which they are a part of the curriculum, a question naturally arises: Why are these programs not found in a larger number of junior colleges?

There are several answers to this question. In the first place many junior colleges were established specifically to offer liberal arts education or preprofessional programs for transfer students. In the first category are a number of colleges operated by religious orders of the Roman Catholic Church, which admit only those who are preparing for the entry into the religious orders. Among the junior colleges that offer nothing but transfer-type liberal arts or preprofessional programs, by far the largest number is composed of private junior colleges. These include church-related and independent schools.

A second reason for the smaller number of junior colleges offering vocational curriculums is the comparatively high cost. The initial per-student cost of building shops and equipping them runs far higher than that for programs in the academic fields. Moreover, the initial cost in no way reflects the total expense of operating vocational programs. There is the constant factor of maintenance, repair, and replacement of machinery. More costs are incurred by the continual improvement of machinery and the constant problem of obsolescence. For example, a recent addition to the junior college vocational curriculum is the data-processing program. The only way in which many colleges can offer this program is to lease the necessary equipment and have it replaced by the manufacturers when it becomes obsolete. Even so, the cost involved is prohibitively high for many junior colleges.

A third reason for the limited popularity of vocational curriculums in junior colleges is found in a principle associated with the operation of such programs. The continued success of the program depends substantially on the degree to which graduates of the programs can find employment. Some junior colleges have, for this reason, limited their offerings to programs of preparation for jobs in which the demand for workers is high. Occupational surveys or data obtained from the office of the nearest employment office are used to gauge demand. Some junior colleges are located in areas in which there is little employment opportunity for most of the typical vocational programs. When this is the case, boards and administrators logically stay out of the field of vocational training.

Community Service

At the outset of this chapter, three general curriculum divisions were listed: general education, preparatory education, and vocational education. These three divisions have been described. Now attention is directed to a fourth division: community service.

In a very real sense, this topic cannot logically be equated with the three divisions just described. Actually, it is implicit in all of them. The student in the public junior college who is permitted the economy of living at home, working part-time at the job he may have had through high school, and taking courses in any or all of the three divisions described is being provided with a community service.

Moreover, many of the educational services which might be classified under this heading are far more informal in organization than any of the more formally structured courses in the first three divisions. A community service may take the form of a short-unit, noncredit course offered in the adult evening school on such topics as flower arrangement, or Christmas-package wrapping. These units are usually greeted with derision by those who are inclined to be critical of junior colleges anyway, yet their value is attested to by the large number of adults who take the courses.

The field of community service is so diffuse, so ephemeral, that the only way the writer has been able to define it to his own satisfaction is by means of a residual approach based on an arbitrary delimitation. On this basis, the community-service program includes all the educational services provided by a junior college over and beyond the regular day program for full-time students.

Because of the more formal structuring of courses in the general, preparatory, and vocational education programs, it is possible to enumerate in specific terms the number of offerings in each of these fields—as, for example, the 95 separate vocational programs listed by junior colleges. It would be impossible to count the offerings in the area of community service. If it were possible to take an inventory of such services, the number and nature of the services would have changed before the census could be completed. The best method is to describe the more frequently found general areas.

Evening school. Probably the most formally structured aspect of community service is the evening school. In this organization will be found many of the offerings of junior colleges described under the first three major divisions. Moreover, as was pointed out earlier, many of those who attend evening school are full-time students who attend classes in the mornings, work on a part-time job in the afternoon, and then return to the evening school to complete their full schedule of work. In addition to these elements of the regular program, however, evening schools attract thousands of adults who attend all kinds of classes for an assortment of reasons. There are those who are working on formal programs to complete interrupted collegiate programs for an associate degree, those who are pursuing a particular interest, and those lonely individuals who find the evening school a satisfying medium for making social contacts.

The variety of programs in the adult evening school is limited only by such factors as the creative imagination of its director, the policy of the junior college, or the physical resources and budget of the institution. Instructors in both credit and noncredit courses include laymen, as well as members of the regular junior college faculty.

The motivations of those who attend are, as has already been noted, widely diversified. Some may be seeking the satisfaction of qualifying for a junior college degree. Others may be taking refresher courses in vocational subjects because of a desire to go back to income-producing employment. Some may wish to acquire new vocational skills in order to move out of a job which is becoming obsolete, or as a basis for advancement to a better job. Some may desire to develop a hobby in the arts or in any of the many crafts. Some may want to get an education in certain fields for the sheer enjoyment of getting an education. In some instances, the motivation might be a desire to acquire a nonvocational skill in such a field as flower arrangement, or more practical information, such as how to fill out an income tax form. The list of motivations is endless, but each motivation has a definite implication: it is strong enough to lure the adult out of his home in the evenings to acquire an education in line with his interests. The junior college which allows him to satisfy his needs is performing a real community service.

Fine arts groups. Another general area of community service is that provided by the various fine arts groups of the junior college. These may take many forms. Choral groups or instrumental groups may give formal recitals in the college auditorium or appear before various men's or women's clubs in the community. They may present formal musicals or operettas, and frequently provide special music for such occasions as Easter or Christmas. The drama department will probably present plays or combine with the music department in the more ambitious productions. The art department may present formal exhibitions or participate cooperatively with other fine arts departments in various activities.

Very often the fine arts groups will work with off-campus groups in public or parochial schools. Children's theater projects are a popular example of such activities. Occasionally, the objective of these groups is to assist in the development of fine arts appreciation among elementary or secondary school pupils through lectures and demonstrations, and sometimes these same opportunities are provided for adults.

Some junior colleges participate in bringing a fine arts series to the community as well as to the junior college students. These may take the form of lecture series, or occasionally, the operation of public forums at which the public is given an opportunity to discuss issues of current interest. Exhibits of paintings, photographs, or other art forms are regularly provided by some junior colleges.

Civic leadership. One role of the junior college faculty in providing community service that is generally overlooked is provided outside the regular classroom and lies beyond professional duties. This service consists of the contributions which these faculty members make to the community as citizens. The junior college faculty member and administrator are the products of a great deal of professional preparation and experience. Except for the junior college, they would not be residents of the community. Thus the contribution they make as citizens of the community is a direct result of the existence of the junior college, and can thus be classified as one of its community services.

Faculty members fill many leadership roles in the community. Their competence is utilized by churches, civic organizations, special-interest clubs, and charitable organizations. Usually, they hold offices in all types of organizations. Very often the special competence of these college personnel is used in other ways by the community. Some colleges maintain a speakers' bureau, listing faculty members and the topics they will discuss in formal presentations. Some communities utilize these special competences of faculty members in advisory or consultative roles.

As with all aspects of community service, the list of services provided by the professional personnel of the college is an extensive one. Some idea of its magnitude may be gained through imagining the loss the community would suffer if the junior college were to close and all its professional personnel were to move away.

CHAPTER IV

Students and Student-Personnel Programs

Student Characteristics

What are junior college students like? Some facts are available to answer this question, and some additional studies are being made which will provide more information. But it may never be possible to arrive at any far-reaching generalizations because of the marked diversity of types of junior colleges and of the students who attend them.

It should be observed that the range of diversity will be reduced as more and more junior colleges apply for and receive admission to regional accrediting associations. Differences among junior colleges, and among junior college students will continue to exist, just as marked differences may be observed among four-year colleges and universities and their students. This diversity has been regarded by some as one of the strengths of higher education in the United States.

Although there is a dearth of authoritative information about junior college students, there is unfortunately no dearth of folklore and myth. The misfortune is that, although all this "information" is without foundation, those who accept it and help to keep it in circulation are frequently persons whose judgment is relied upon by others seeking enlightenment. Before examining the few facts known about junior college students, let us consider the myths which have developed over the years.

One of these appears to be particularly popular with many faculty members in four-year colleges and universities. This stereotype represents the junior college student as inferior, by nature, to students in the four-year colleges and universities. This view persists in spite of the fact that countless studies over almost a half-century have destroyed any foundation for it. The viewpoint is difficult to condone when it is realized that many who hold it are respectable scholars in their own fields and would condemn anyone who so persistently ignored established facts.

A second myth, closely related to the one just described, holds that the only justification for the junior colleges is the provision of vocational education. On this basis, two-year colleges are considered to go "beyond their depth" when they offer academic programs. Those who hold this view regard all the "misguided" students who "blunder into" junior colleges as vocational students. In its extreme manifestation, this viewpoint judges junior college students as beyond the province of academic respectability. This view, too, is without foundation.

A third phase of this same viewpoint—one held by the ultraconservatives—regards the junior college student as typical of those for whom further education is a waste of time. Those who hold this notion range from persons who regard higher education as a privilege strictly reserved for those who can pay for it in a private institution to those who are generally opposed to any undertaking that will place an additional obligation on the taxpayer. This kind of opposition refuses to accept any arguments based on the exploitation of human resources as a means of national progress.

Still another phase of the folklore concludes that all college students are essentially alike. In some states, this view leads to the establishment of policies which forbid the creation of a public junior college within a specified number of miles of an existing four-year college. This oversimplification of the range of educational purposes of prospective college students is patently without foundation. Its only possible justification—the protection of existing four-year colleges against competition—loses its validity in the face of the phenomenal increase in the number of young people currently seeking admission to college.

There are many other myths pertaining to the nature of junior college students. All have one thing in common with those which have been described: they are groundless.

Ability range. One fact which *is* known about junior college students concerns their wide range of ability, aptitude, motivation, and orientation. As was intimated at the outset of this chapter, the diversity among junior colleges will produce wide or narrow ranges of student performance in individual schools, but when the students are considered in the aggregate, the range is much wider than that which prevails among students of four-year colleges and universities.

Junior college students with the greatest ability compare favorably with the most able students in four-year colleges. Differences usually appear when the less able of the two groups are compared. The less able in the junior college drop substantially below the less able in the four-year colleges. It is quite natural to expect that the computation of a mean or a median for the junior college student will be lower than that for students in four-year colleges.

The contrast in ranges of ability between students in junior college and those in four-year colleges, and the consequent contrast in the mean or median ability, is likely to become even more pronounced. Many four-year colleges and universities are controlling their increased enrollments through the imposition of progressively higher admission standards. Unless the junior colleges adopt similar policies, which seems highly unlikely, the four-year schools will force more and more students into the junior colleges. Although the increases occasioned by this factor will certainly not entail poor academic risks, they will include students unable to meet the rising admission standards of the four-year colleges.

This characteristic of junior college students has definite implications for the instructional program in junior colleges, and for actual and prospective faculty members in these colleges. In those junior colleges in which there is a wide range of ability among the students, there is a strong probability that this same characteristic will prevail in the individual classes. This condition, as was pointed out in Chapter III, will necessitate greater instructional efficiency if the junior college takes seriously its educational obligation to all students admitted.

Part-time employment. A second characteristic of junior college students is the large number who earn part or all of the money for college expenses while attending college. This characteristic is not uniformly predominant: it varies according to the type of junior college. On the basis of figures compiled from *American Junior Colleges,*[1] over 40 per cent of the students in local or district junior colleges display it, while in the church-related junior colleges only 15 per cent do; in independent junior colleges, 30 per cent; in state

---

[1] Edmund Gleazer, Jr. (ed.), *American Junior Colleges,* 6th ed. (Washington, D.C.: American Council on Education, 1964).

junior colleges, 26.6 per cent; and in branch public junior colleges, 15.9 per cent.

It should be recalled that the cost of attending local and district type junior colleges is generally smaller than that for attending most of the other types of institutions. If this were not the case, it is probable that a large number of students who are earning enough to pay for part or all of their college expenses would find attendance impossible. It should also be kept in mind that a further reduction in cost is made possible for students in local and district junior colleges by their living at home. Only 4.3 per cent of these students live in college dormitories.

The large number of students who are earning part or all of their college expenses is responsible for certain organizational patterns in the daily schedules in the junior colleges. Two distinct patterns may be observed.

In some junior colleges, particularly in the local or district classification, the daily schedule for most of the students concludes around 1:00 P.M. Many students then go to part-time jobs. In many instances, these students return for additional classes in the adult evening school.

A second pattern of schedule organization involves starting the day at the customary opening time of the individual school and continuing until 10:00 P.M. or later. In this situation, there is no semi-independent adult evening school. Instead, instructors are employed and assigned a full load of classwork (usually fifteen semester hours, or the equivalent) with a schedule worked out within the confines of a fourteen-hour or longer day.

Curriculum followed. Another means of classifying junior college students is based on the curriculum they follow. In this classification are three divisions: transfer students, terminal students, and adult students. The first two types are full-time students; the third are part-time students. Although this classification of junior college students is used more frequently than the two described previously, it is far less definitive. First, it provides little or no information about the characteristics of the three types of students to permit distinguishing among them. Second, there is a marked inconstancy among the three types. Actually a far greater number of students classify themselves as transfer students than do eventually transfer to a four-year college. This classification is not so much an act of self-designation as it is an observation of the nature of the courses which students elect. By this process, a substantial number who would normally be classified as transfer students are actually terminal students in that they terminate their formal schooling at some time during the junior college years.

The classification of adult students is also marked by inconsistency. Certainly, not all students who attend evening classes fall into this category. It has already been explained that many of these students are merely rounding out a school day which began in the morning. Many of those who are genuinely part-time students will transfer to a four-year college after compiling the required number of credit hours.

Finally, terminal students present the same lack of consistency implied in their classification. Many of these whose original intention was to terminate their formal schooling with the junior college will change their plans and decide to go on. The gradual relaxation of transfer requirements in many four-year colleges operates to facilitate such a change in plans. For these reasons, although the classifications *transfer, terminal,* and *adult* are used most frequently, the student of the junior college must recognize that their applicability is often not justified by actual practice.

Student-Personnel Programs

Reference has already been made to the fact that the preponderant majority of students attending local or district junior colleges live at home. On the basis of the computation made from the identified source,[2] 95.7 per cent of the students in these colleges live at home. At the other extreme are the students in church-related junior colleges, 73 per cent of whom live on campus. Other types of junior colleges, and the percentage of students living on campus include: state, 43.7 per cent; branch public, 7.6 per cent; and independent, 45.6 per cent.

The conditions described by this consideration of the residence of junior college students have definite implications for the nature of student-personnel programs developed in these educational institutions. Any college exercises a far greater contact with the stu-

---

[2] *Ibid.*

dents who live on campus than with those who are away from the campus a greater part of each day. This increased contact makes possible a more effective operation of the student-personnel services. It does not necessarily follow, however, that the opportunity thus presented is exploited to the fullest.

The opportunity for operating a more effective program is particularly noticeable in certain areas of the student-personnel program. Among these are residence relations in dormitories, health services, student activities, and student orientation. Each of these will be considered more in detail.

Two conditions mitigate against the maximum of success of the student-personnel program. These need examination before the details of the program itself can be considered. Both factors are usually present in junior colleges maintaining residence halls, although one is found in other junior colleges as well. These factors concern (1) the relation of resident students and day students, and (2) the "suitcase" college.

The factor involving the relationship of day students and resident students may be observed in many aspects of campus life, but probably nowhere will its effect be more apparent than in many phases of the student activities program. Students who commute daily to the junior college usually return to their homes after their daily schedule of classes is completed. Resident students, on the other hand, are on the campus most of the time. Student activities meetings for resident students are frequently scheduled at night, after the dinner hour, as a matter of convenience. Quite often, day students are eliminated from participation in these activities simply because they don't care to remain on campus until the scheduled meeting time—or, having gone home, don't care to make a trip back to the campus.

As was indicated, this factor occasionally operates on campuses without residence halls. In these instances, the students are divided among those who are employed at part-time jobs and those who are not. The former sometimes find themselves at a distinct disadvantage in trying to participate in student activities scheduled at times inconvenient to them.

The "suitcase" factor is usually found in junior colleges in which the resident students come from homes within reasonable commuting distance of the college. For them, the end of their last class of the week is the signal to set out for home. A mass exodus from the campus may be observed at that time. The weekend on the campus is frequently a rather dull time for the few students whose homes are so far away they cannot join the exodus. The "suitcase" students return to the campus en masse on the evening before the resumption of regular classes.

This "suitcase" factor presents a serious problem for those responsible for planning the social activities of the college. Because major social events are normally scheduled for the weekend, the situation of the large number who go home must be taken into consideration. There is also the problem of planning recreational activities for the relatively small number of students who remain on the campus over the weekend.

It should be reiterated that the two factors described are not present on all junior college campuses. Where they are present, however, they are of sufficient magnitude to create serious planning problems.

There is a seeming disposition on the part of many in the junior college field to regard student-personnel services as consisting exclusively of guidance and counseling. Although of the many junior colleges in which this view is held fulfill the other functions of student-personnel programs, the failure to link these into a well-coordinated program detracts from the effectiveness of the total operation.

This report will concern itself with the following aspects of this program: (1) selection of students, (2) recruitment, (3) admission, (4) personnel testing, (5) orientation, (6) records, (7) scholarships, (8) loans, (9) guidance and counseling, (10) housing, (11) health services, (12) student activities, (13) discipline, (14) placement, (15) follow-up, (16) research and on-going studies. Because there is a paucity of definitive information about the status of these functions in junior colleges in general, descriptive treatment will concern itself with the various practices found under each of the functions.

Specialized personnel. One justified generalization is related to the use of specialized personnel in the student-personnel program. Although many junior colleges have not recognized adequately the interrelatedness of the several aspects of the student-personnel program, there are few—if any—of these educational institutions in which most of the functions do not operate. In the colleges with smaller enrollments, the responsibilities related to the several functions are, from necessity, clustered around a relatively small number of administrative positions. As the junior college enrollment increases, specialized personnel are usually employed and assigned responsibility for a single function. Coordination of the program presents a less difficult task in the larger junior colleges where a single function is assigned to a responsible administrative office, and where planning is facilitated by conferences of the specialized officials.

Selection of students.   The selection of prospective students for a given junior college should bear a positive correlation to the institution's over-all purposes. If such purposes are carefully stated, they exist to indicate which students may be served by the college and which cannot.

The way in which this process of selection operates varies. The junior college with an "open door" policy sets an absolute minimum—graduation from high school—for admission. In other junior colleges, the process of selection is becoming increasingly more rigorous. The latter policy is typical of privately controlled junior colleges, in which a plan of limiting total enrollment has been adopted. In these cases, the selective factor is most often that of demonstrated scholarship, or a hidden economic factor revealed in increased tuition costs.

Recruitment of students.   Practices used in recruiting prospective students for junior colleges vary widely among the institutions. Among the many practices, six have been chosen for description.

The first recruiting practices involves the sending out of field representatives. This practice is far more common among the privately controlled junior colleges than among those under public control. Some colleges employ full-time representatives. In some other institutions, the work is confined primarily to the summer months and regular faculty members. Field contacts usually involve either visits to the prospective students in their homes or talks with groups of students at their secondary schools.

The procedure of talking with groups of students is facilitated by a second practice followed in some states. A "college day" will be scheduled by the high school administrators or counselors, and all colleges in the state or area will be notified and invited to send representatives. In such instances, provision is made for the representative of a given college to talk with the students who have previously indicated an interest in that college.

Another fairly common practice among many junior colleges is the sending of musical ensembles to appear at high school assembly programs. These groups are often accompanied by a representative of the college, who will speak briefly about the college. This practice differs from the first two described in that it seldom provides an opportunity for "committed" students to sign an application blank—an opportunity generally provided in the first two practices.

A fourth practice which appears to be increasing in popularity involves bringing groups of prospective students to the campus of the junior college. The students may be winners of some form of competition in music or science. Or they may have been invited to attend a special performance of the junior college drama group. Sometimes the college simply holds an open house.

Church-related junior colleges frequently rely on ministers of the denomination sponsoring the college to provide leads for follow-up interviews by field representatives of the college or actually to recruit students. Some publicity for the college is also provided by fund-raising campaigns conducted in the churches.

Another practice used in recruitment concerns activities of alumni groups. Quite often this procedure is used by colleges which draw their students from a wide geographical area. The president of the college will schedule visits with alumni groups to tell them of new developments at the college, to receive suggestions from them, and to learn of prospective students.

Admission of students. The procedure of formally admitting students to junior colleges carries with it the responsibility for determining whether all admission requirements have been met, and whether the fees charged by the college have been paid. The student may participate in a standardized testing program, and will be helped to select the courses he will take for the first semester or quarter.

As is true of all aspects of the student-personnel program, the admissions function varies from junior college to junior college, but a general trend may be observed. This is the trend toward improving the first impression entering students receive of the college in which they are about to begin their post-high school work.

The college registrar has traditionally been regarded as an unpleasant person, totally devoid of any humanitarian strains, who finds his nearest approach to happiness in the rigid enforcement of regulations which seem frequently to operate to the disadvantage of the student. This traditional concept, like so many of a similar nature, is not borne out in fact. That there are some unpleasant registrars is doubtless true, but no more than there are unpleasant presidents, deans, teachers, and even students.

On the other hand, the registrar was and is charged with the performance of certain duties, and his power to deviate from the admission standards is very limited. Since the enforcement of regulations occasionally works to the disadvantage of a particular student, it may be suspected that some of the adverse criticisms heaped on registrars probably had their origin in frustrated students.

The responsibility of the registrar has been expanded beyond a mere check on whether students meet entrance requirements. A new position is emerging in many junior colleges as well as in four-year colleges and universities. This is the position generally called *the admissions officer*. His responsibility encompasses the expanding admission concept—a concept which takes into consideration the extreme importance of helping the new student get a good start in his college work, thereby avoiding the initial misunderstanding which delays his full transition into college life.

Personnel testing. Reference has been made earlier to the incidence of standardized tests which often is a feature of admission procedures. These tests are increasing in junior colleges, both in the number of institutions using them and in the variety of tests administered. Although the testing program is part of the admission procedure, it warrants separate consideration.

One phase of standardized testing which is being used increasingly in junior colleges involves tests which prospective students take while still in high school. The scores made on such tests become a part of the high school transcript which junior colleges require as a prerequisite for admission. The tests required vary from institution to institution. Currently they are required only by a minority of all junior colleges.

The test scores just described apply typically to high school graduates. Most junior colleges recognize for admission a second type of student, who most frequently is not a high school graduate. These students are usually admitted on the basis of having attained a certain chronological age, frequently twenty-one or over, and may be required to submit supplementary evidence in the form of high school equivalency test scores. The well-known General Education Development Test is often specified.

Junior colleges are using, with increasing frequency, placement tests in such academic areas as English, mathematics, and foreign languages. Whenever it is possible to have the scores available in time, they are used in educational guidance for entering students, in sectioning classes according to student ability, and occasionally as a basis for organizing honors courses in certain academic fields.

The practice, adopted in a few four-year colleges, of using placement-test scores as a qualification for advanced standing has not appeared in junior colleges. The reason lies largely in the matter of protecting prospective transfer students from loss of credit in the institution to which he transfers. It is probable that, when the four-year colleges relax their policies in regard to this practice, placement-test scores will find still another use in the junior colleges, as a basis for advanced standing.

Many junior colleges administer psychological examinations to students as a basis for computing intelligence quotients. The I.Q. then become a part of the student's permanent record and is used in counseling.

Another type of test used for counseling is the vocational-interest inventory. It is probable that such tests are administered most often at the request of an individual student, or a counselor, or a college department. They are not used generally as a part of the battery of tests given to the students at the time of their admission.

Although most junior colleges limit the number of standardized tests to those from which the scores will be used actually for valid purposes, some institutions occasionally go beyond this limit. It is unfortunate when this is done, because it often results in a loss of respect for the student-personnel program. Testing merely for the sake of testing cannot be justified.

Student orientation. Junior colleges, like other collegiate institutions, recognize that the transition from high school to college involves the student in a sharply different environment. In high school he accounted for his presence from the beginning of the daily schedule in the morning to the end of the schedule in the afternoon. In college, his presence is accounted for only during the time the classes for which he enrolled are meeting. Orientation programs have been developed as a part of the student-personnel programs to assist new students in making this transition. As with other aspects of the program, practices vary widely.

In some junior colleges, the orientation program is condensed into a period of not more than two or three days. The students are kept going at a rapid pace throughout most of this time. They attend assemblies or conferences; there may be talks by the college administrators or by upperclassmen. The new students may be introduced to the faculty through the process of having faculty members stand briefly as their names are called.

Tours of the campus (if it is large enough to be toured) are arranged under the leadership of sophomore students. A trip to the library is sometimes included, with the librarian pointing out the various features, explaining the services, and discoursing briefly on library schedules and rules.

Sometime in this brief period, students may be assembled in large rooms to take standardized tests. If the test scores are to be used in counseling students about course selection, this testing period is scheduled early enough so that the papers may be scored for such use.

On campuses where there are residence halls, room assignments may be made during orientation. In these cases, informal talks are frequently made by house mothers, and the nature of dormitory government may be explained. This phase usually includes information about dining facilities, and rules about the use of these facilities.

Somewhere along the line, student handbooks will be distributed. These handbooks usually contain a résumé of most of the topics that have been discussed with the students. Also found in the handbook will be information about student activities and a miscellany of additional features such as the college colors, the words of the alma mater, the college mascot, and a word or two about the intercollegiate athletic program, if there is one.

Other junior colleges conduct their orientation activities at a more leisurely pace. In many, the orientation will be incorporated into a course, credit or noncredit, in which the new students are taken through many of the topics previously described, but in a classroom situation. When the orientation is presented through regularly organized courses, the classes frequently are scheduled to meet for one hour per week, and class enrollments are kept small enough to permit discussion of the topics by the students.

When regular orientation courses are offered, they are required for all entering students, and may deal with one of two general topics, or with a combination of both. One topic is identical with that which underlies the short orientation: an introduction to life in the junior college which the students have entered. The other topic, found in some orientation courses, concerns an introduction to the period of late adolescence or early adulthood when such important decisions are made as those which pertain to the selection of a mate, the selection of a vocation, or the selection of an academic area for concentration.

It was noted earlier that in those junior colleges having both resident and day students, the orientation aspect of the student-personnel program was often affected. One way in which this influence may be observed relates to those phases of the orientation program scheduled at times inconvenient for attendance by day students. There is another phase, however, which is even more significant.

Many junior colleges which present the condensed-form orientation program described undertake to assemble all the new students two or three days prior to the regular registration period. This undertaking is always a difficult one, and seldom is it completely satisfactory as measured by the proportion of the total number of new students who attend. Often, among those absent are the day students, particularly those living near enough to the campus to have been told by older students about the questionable benefit of these orientation periods. Another factor enters the picture for many of the day students. This is the period of transition for many from full-time jobs to part-time jobs, and the eagerness to prolong the period of full-time employment as long as possible to increase the amount earned.

Student records. In commenting on student-personnel services in two-year colleges, Medsker lists good records of students' academic programs as one of the elements of strength.[3] The conclusion, however, might well have been predicted because a satisfactory set of academic records is indispensable to the certification of credits for transfer purposes. Carelessness in this important area would become immediately apparent, and the gravity of omitting any significant portion of the records would be a severe blow to the professional reputation of the institution.

Many junior colleges keep a set of personnel records in addition to the students' permanent academic records. This practice facilitates the use of pertinent personnel data by those responsible for counseling without risking the misplacement or possible alteration of the permanent records. When this procedure is followed, the personnel records are usually in the form of folders. Usually the folders themselves are so arranged that needed information may be entered on the inside of the folder itself. Moreover, the folder makes possible the deposit of notes on student conferences and other such information.

Scholarships. All types of junior colleges offer scholarships. These vary greatly in the purpose for which they are awarded. Some junior colleges make a blanket offer to all the high school valedictorians in the state in which the junior college is located. Some church-related junior colleges offer full or part scholarships to the children of ministers of the religious denomination which sponsors the junior college. Scholarships are awarded for the purpose of developing or maintaining certain student activities, such as athletics or musical organizations.

Methods of awarding scholarships also vary. Quite often, as in the case of awards made to first-year students for their second year, the awards are made by faculty committees. In other instances, when the award is based on demonstrated performance, the scholarship winner is certified by the high school from which he comes.

The nature of the award also varies from junior college to junior college. In many cases, the scholarship consists of a mere bookkeeping arrangement in the remission of fees or tuition. In other instances, the amount of the scholarship is given in cash and spent by the winner for his college expenses.

Many junior colleges have a species of award called *work schol-*

---

[3] Leland L. Medsker, *The Junior College: Progress and Prospect* (New York: McGraw-Hill Book Company, 1960), p. 162.

arships. The person receiving such a scholarship is employed part-time by the college and either paid a certain amount, often computed on an hourly rate, or is given a remission of part of his college expenses, or receives his meals free.

American Junior Colleges[4] lists the number of scholarship winners in junior colleges and the total values of the scholarships. The data are based on the academic year, 1961–62, and are exclusive of work scholarships. No attempt is made to list the purposes for which the scholarships were given, or whether they represent grants in cash or remission of part or all of the college expenses.

District junior colleges award the largest number of scholarships, 6554, but rank second to church-related junior colleges in the total value of such awards. District junior college total scholarship value is $1,005,608, while the total value of the scholarship awards of church-related junior colleges is $1,290,693.

Probably a better basis for comparing the scholarship status of the several types of junior colleges is the average size of the scholarships. To arrive at this figure, the total value of the scholarships was divided by the number of award winners. If these figures are used, a sharper difference may be observed between the district junior colleges, in which the average is $153.43, and the church-related institution, in which the average is $248.93. Data for each of the types of junior colleges is presented in Table 1.

TABLE 1

SCHOLARSHIPS AWARDED BY JUNIOR COLLEGES

TYPE	SCHOLARSHIPS		
	Total Number	Total Value	Average Value
Local public	5430	$ 721,662	$132.90
District public	6554	1,005,608	153.53
Branch public	1255	257,971	205.55
State	1441	198,770	137.94
Church-related	5185	1,290,693	248.93
Independent	1910	912,621	477.81

Student loans. The principle of maintaining loan funds to assist students finance educational costs is well established in junior colleges. The principle of regarding such transactions as aspects of student personnel programs is less well established. In many of the

---

[4] Gleazer, *op. cit.*

junior colleges, this activity is handled directly by the business office; in these instances, the major consideration is typically given to the security of the borrower rather than to a realistic appraisal of the student's financial needs. One of the reasons for this situation is the paucity of specialized counseling services. A realistic assessment of financial need frequently reveals the deficiency to be a lack of understanding of the magnitude of need. Effective assistance to students in such matters requires a type of counseling which includes thorough familiarity with personal financing. It is a responsibility in which the counselor should have specialized knowledge. Only then will the student obtain the type of help he needs.

Just as practices vary in the administration of loan funds, so is there variance among junior colleges in the number of users of loan funds, and in the total amounts loaned. On the basis of types of junior colleges, the largest number of borrowers are enrolled in local public junior colleges: 6425.[5] When the number of borrowers

TABLE 2

SCHOLARSHIPS RECEIVED BY JUNIOR COLLEGE STUDENTS

TYPE	SCHOLARSHIPS		
	Number of Borrowers	Total Amount Borrowed	Average Amount Per Borrower
Local public	6425	$ 491,306	$ 76.47
District public	5526	892,969	161.59
Branch public	217	71,834	329.40
State	1940	538,720	277.69
Church-related	3062	1,192,050	389.30
Independent	1932	599,673	310.35

in this type of junior college is divided into the total amount loaned—$491,306, the average loan thus computed, $76.47, is the smallest average in any of the types. The largest amount loaned, $1,192,050, and the largest average size loan, $389.30 for each of 3062 borrowers, is in the church-related college. The status of loans in each of the different types of junior college is shown in Table 2.

Guidance and counseling. In the days when the number of students enrolled in any given college was small, when the curriculum was devoted to liberal arts with no elective choices for students

---

[5] *Ibid.*

to make, and before the entry of vocational preparation at the college level, there was little or no need for guidance and counseling as these terms are currently employed. True, there was guidance and counseling of a sort, but this consisted primarily of informal chats between teachers and students in an environment so intimate and restricted that everyone could know everyone. Times have changed.

The homogeneity of yesterday's student body has changed to heterogeneity. The number of specialized courses in the third and fourth years of the undergraduate college has increased substantially. Even in the first and second years, the entry of many new curriculums—vocational, for example—has increased the number of courses materially. Thus, the problem of making a wise choice of desirable curriculums and courses has become a serious one, making obvious the need for assistance from a guidance and counseling program.

Very few undergraduate colleges offer vocational programs of two years or less in duration. The presence of this feature among most of the junior colleges creates for many students at this level the need for help in selecting among these several programs.

It was pointed out earlier in this chapter that students in junior colleges usually presented a wider range of characteristics than those of many of the four-year colleges. In its earlier context, this circumstance was related to the need for superior instructional efficiency, but it also carries an implication for effective guidance and counseling programs.

These student bodies usually include some persons who lack prerequisite qualities for successful performance in some phases of the junior college curriculum. Some are deficient in academic aptitude, or orientation, or motivation. Although some of these deficiencies may be overcome in the classroom by superior instruction, the causes for others are more deeply rooted. Frequently, these causes can be eliminated by the efforts of a well-prepared counselor. In a few cases, the causes will yield only to psychiatric care.

The need for guidance and counseling has been intensified by the marked progress in the general area of mental health. Deviate behavior, once attributed mainly to perversity of character, is seen now as symptomatic of emotional disturbance. If the condition is not serious, it may be remedied by the work of an efficient counselor. If the condition is serious, the competence of the counselor enables him to recognize the significance of symptoms, and thus to refer the case to a psychiatrist or to a school psychologist. Finally, the progress that has been made in the several fields of diagnostical testing has increased the need for trained counselors. The technical competence needed for administering many of these tests appropriately, and for interpreting test scores intelligently, is frequently not possessed by the regular classroom teacher.

From the considerations described in the paragraphs immediately preceding, it may be concluded that junior college students have a very real need for the assistance provided by a counseling and guidance program. In the face of this need, a question arises: How best can this help be provided? Before looking at the very general features comprising an answer to this question, one additional factor should be examined—the nature of counseling needs in terms of the relative sophistication of the counselor.

Implicit in the preceding description of factors underlying the justification of a program of guidance and counseling is the relative complexity of the problems which students need help in solving. Reference was made to the desirability, in some cases, of psychiatric help. In other cases, the student merely needs someone who will "hear him out" on some topic that is confusing him. It was pointed out that the interpretation of some kinds of test or inventory scores requires substantial expertness on the part of the counselor. A similar need exists for a broad understanding of the requirements for entry into and the nature of a vast number of occupational fields and four-year colleges.

The various kinds of competence required for effective counseling suggest that the general features of counseling and guidance services should be considered. The description of organization, structure, and staff must also take into account the size of the junior college as a factor determining the number of specialized positions. In the smaller junior colleges, this number will be proportionately smaller, requiring a combination of responsibilities in one position.

If the junior college is to develop a satisfactory guidance and counseling program, at least one position in this field must be filled by a well-trained person. The responsibility for developing the program will devolve upon this person, and although the magnitude of the program may be severely restricted by limitations of time and staff, there will nevertheless be assurance that the policies adopted and practices followed are consistent with the best principles of a good student-personnel program.

Faculty members constitute an active part of a junior college student-personnel program. Two conditions must be kept in mind concerning their activity: (1) they will provide part-time service, while their major loyalty is most likely to be given to their classroom responsibilities; and (2) their degree of professional competence in this area of junior college service will probably be small. In spite of the factors which limit their usefulness, there are certain aspects of the counseling program in which the contribution of faculty members will be satisfactory. One example of this is the help given students in working out their schedules of courses for succeeding semesters or quarters.

The two phases of the structure of the student-personnel program which have been described—the well-trained director of the program, and the members of the faculty working under the service limitations noted—in one sense make up the top and the bottom of the organization. Many positions will be found in between these two. For example, it may be decided to staff the organization with a certain number of professionally trained counselors to work with students on more serious problems. Another example would be a professional staff charged with the responsibility of the testing program.

The larger institutions most often place the student-personnel program under the administrative control of a Director of Student Personnel, a Dean of Students, or an official known by some similar title. In these cases, this official will be charged with administering the entire program, and counseling responsibility as such will be assigned to other members of his staff.

Currently, in spite of the urgent need for the guidance and counseling services in junior colleges, the development of such programs is markedly deficient. External evidence may easily be found to affirm that recognition of the need for counseling is widespread. As Medsker points out:

> A narrow view is often taken on what constitutes counseling. In many colleges the view prevailed that when a student could be assisted in arranging a program of classes which met his personal

desires and also met requirements of transfer to a senior college, the major task of counseling had been fulfilled. Important as this service is, it does not include the more important task of helping the student to make certain of his occupational preference by various rational means; to make a wise choice of the next higher institution, if there is to be one; to analyze his achievement record in relation to his aptitude; and to solve some of the personal problems which may be affecting his academic or social adjustment. These are only some of the other aspects of counseling for which competent assistance should be available.[6]

Student housing.   Based on computations made from the data for 1961–62 in *American Junior College*,[7] approximately 44 per cent of the 655 junior colleges listed had dormitories. The incidence of dormitories varied from a low of 5 per cent in local public junior colleges to a high of 87 per cent in church-related colleges. Other types of junior colleges classified with dormitories are: district public, 39 per cent; branch public, 18 per cent; state, 70 per cent; and independent, 62 per cent. Although the colleges with dormitories form a significant proportion of all junior colleges, of the total number of students enrolled in junior colleges, only 17 per cent live in dormitories. Actually, this percentage is based on the total of full-time students. If the total included both full-time and part-time students, the percentage would drop much lower.

A variance is also found in the percentage of students living in dormitories in the several types of junior colleges. As would be expected, the type of junior college with the highest percentage of students living in dormitories is the church-related school. Seventy-three per cent of the students in this type of junior college live in dormitories. The type with the lowest percentage of such students is the local public where only 0.4 per cent are so housed. Other types and the percentages are: district public, 9 per cent; branch public, 8 per cent; state, 44 per cent; and independent, 46 per cent.

From these computations, it may be concluded that the factor of student housing as an aspect of student-personnel programs is really significant in only three types of junior colleges: state, church-related, and independent. The relative infrequency of residence halls on the campuses of the other three types indicates that most

[6] Medsker, *op. cit.*, p. 163.
[7] Gleazer, *op. cit.*

of them have no need to develop this service in their student-personnel program.

Four important considerations, from the standpoint of student-personnel services, are encountered in junior college dormitories, (1) adjustment to group living, (2) counseling, (3) discipline, and (4) the development of study habits. Student-personnel programs are organized to provide assistance along these lines.

Many junior colleges have found student self-government in the residence halls to be a valuable element in dealing with all these considerations. Student leaders, often called *proctors,* work with the residence counselors and with committees of dormitory students in devising plans which will help achieve the conditions desired. Student conferences in the residence halls permit the participation of all the residents in discussion of problems of the residence hall or the entire college.

Health services. As was pointed out in an earlier chapter, the student-personnel aspect of health services applies primarily to junior colleges in which a substantial portion of the students enrolled are resident students. There is no disposition to suggest that such services are not needed by day students, but the very fact that all day students live off the campus reduces the need for the college to supply such services.

Health service, as an aspect of the student-personnel program, may generally be divided into two major aspects: (1) the record of the student's medical history and of a physical examination conducted a reasonably short time before the student's admission (these become part of the student's personnel folder); and (2) the provision of facilities and staff to care for student illness or injury. Although other services may be provided, and there are many ramifications to the two listed, these two constitute the most frequently found health services.

The student's health record is of importance in many aspects of the student's on-campus life. It should become a useful source in counseling, particularly that part which is devoted to helping a student with his personal problems. It is also vital to the operation of a desirable physical education program. It is valuable in vocational counseling and, sometimes, in effective placement service after the student leaves college.

The need for staff and facilities to care for students who are ill or are injured is obvious. The staff in smaller junior colleges usually includes a registered nurse who is available at all times, with arrangements made for a local physician to be called in when needed. Usually an infirmary will be provided, or quarters in residence halls set aside for students who need treatment. First-aid equipment is also kept available. Some junior colleges substitute a working arrangement with a local hospital for the maintenance of infirmaries.

Student activities.   The student-activities phase of the student-personnel program comprises several categories of organizations. This is one part of the program that is generally conceded by students of the junior college to have been developed satisfactorily. Included in the categories are: student government, honor organizations, service organizations, special-interest clubs, fine arts organizations, student publications, and social clubs. If interpreted broadly, these titles of categories include most, if not all, the types of student activities.

In a very real sense, intercollegiate athletic teams should be included under the heading of *student activities.* In many junior colleges which field athletic teams, this phase of the program exists apart from the student-personnel program.

The significance of the student-activities organizations varies from junior college to junior college, as do the individual organizations in a given junior college. Student government, for example, occupies an influential position in some junior colleges, while in others its chief excuse for existence is to justify student elections. The same situation exists in regard to student honor organizations.

Student activities, theoretically part of the student-personnel program, do not always function as such. This lack of coordination frequently prevails in other parts of the program. Sponsors of activities frequently have no part whatever in the over-all planning of the student-personnel services, and act in complete independence of it. For this reason, the contribution of these activities to the effectiveness of the student-personnel program may be negligible.

Discipline.   Most junior colleges have established regulations to govern the on-campus conduct of students. Because violations of these regulations occur, provisions are made to deal with the disciplinary cases. These provisions are generally regarded as a part of the student-personnel program.

It is a rather common practice to publish regulations for student conduct in the student handbook (mentioned earlier in another context). Copies of these handbooks, sometimes published by the student government organization, are distributed to all students.

The assignment of staff responsibility for the enforcement of the regulations is usually made to officials called *the dean of men* and *the dean of women*. Many junior colleges have disciplinary committees composed of representatives of the faculty and of the students; these committees pass on alleged violations of the regulations. Their conclusions are made in terms of recommendations for action, if they find that there is sufficient basis to justify the charges made. Implementation of their decision is placed in the hands of some member of the professional staff, frequently one or the other of the two deans. Sound administrative practice keeps the chief administrator informed as to the recommended action, and accords him the right to veto or to modify the decision if, in his judgment, such alteration is needed.

One principle observed by some of the student-personnel programs requires a separation of the functions of counselor and disciplinarian. The theory underlying this principle is that the rapport necessary between the counselor and the student is diminished— if not actually destroyed—if the counselor is at the same time the judge, jury, and executioner.

Placement services. Vocational placement services are maintained by many junior colleges. As is true of other aspects of student-personnel services, practices vary materially among the institutions. In some junior colleges, the responsibility is discharged by one or more persons who work full-time. A very common practice among junior colleges is for this work to be delegated to a representative or representatives of the several vocational departments. In some junior colleges, placement is considered to include assistance given to students in securing jobs designed to help defray part or all of their college expenses. When so considered, the service includes not only jobs on campus (sometimes called *work scholarships*), but also includes help in securing off-campus employment.

Follow-up. Although follow-up is almost always included in any listing of services which should be provided in the student-personnel program, very few junior colleges do little more than a minimum of such work. Few adverse criticisms will be voiced against the practice. The chief reason for lack of performance appears to be the reluctance or inability to expend the extra effort, time, and money required.

One aspect of follow-up that is fairly frequently found in junior colleges is the securing information of the academic records of the students who have transferred to four-year colleges. The cause for the frequency of this practice may be found in one or the other of two conditions, or in a combination of both.

The success of transfer students in the four-year colleges has long been regarded as an important criterion for judging the excellence of a junior college. For this reason, junior college administrators like to have this information. Moreover, the information is of importance in the relations of the junior colleges with their respective regional accrediting associations.

A second cause for the satisfactory condition of this phase of follow-up is found in the policies of the four-year colleges to which the junior college students transfer. Many of these colleges, as a matter of regular procedure, keep an active file on the performance record of all transfer students, regardless of the educational institutions from which they come. As a result of this policy, the information is readily available, and it requires little extra effort to pass it along to the junior colleges.

Follow-up of graduates who do not transfer to four-year colleges is far less common. The rate of follow-up activity drops even more sharply for those students who either drop out during a semester or a quarter, or who withdraw from the junior college before graduation. Some junior colleges do undertake to follow up on such students, and some make every effort possible to provide an exit interview to every student who withdraws.

Research. Experience over the years has taught that certain information about students is indispensable for the best operation of a student personnel program. Although the type of information regarded as significant varies widely, and often in a manner that is consistent with the institutional purposes of the junior college, some illustrations of types of information desired may be cited. In addition to the performance records of students while in the junior college, data are collected which reveal such things as where the students come from, their performance record in high school, the socioeconomic group they represent, the number of students who stay in the junior college until they are graduated, and the major causes for premature withdrawals.

Information of the type described is of value in obtaining a better understanding of the characteristics of the individuals who make up the student body. The value of this information is its usefulness in forming policy and developing curriculum, and as a basis for counseling. It has one additional value when it is coupled with information about the operation of the program: it provides a basis for the continual evaluation that is necessary to assure that student-personnel services are always at the peak of efficiency. Such evaluation is done by all too few junior colleges.

CHAPTER V

Professional Staff

Characteristics

The professional staff of the junior college, as the term will be used in this chapter, refers to faculty members and administrators. *American Junior Colleges*,[1] lists a total of 24,082 staff members, or 21,072 faculty members and 3010 administrators. The ratio of teachers to administrators is approximately eight to one (computed in terms of full-time equivalents), according to the *Junior College Directory*.[2]

Certain characteristics of junior college staffs as a whole are reported in *American Junior Colleges*. On the basis of the total number of staff members reported, five types of junior colleges have a sufficient number to justify comparison. These are: local, district, and state; and church-related and independent.

Local junior colleges lead, with 15,491 full-time and part-time staff members; the district junior college is second with 10,577. The three other types, in order of their total full-time and part-time staff members, and the number in each, are: independent (4072), church-related (3768), and state (1824).

The local public junior colleges rank highest in the number of part-time staff members reported: 6857 or 42.8 per cent of the total mentioned in the preceding paragraph. Many of the local junior colleges are located on the high school campus, and many of its staff members are shared with the high school. As a consequence,

---

[1] Edmund J. Gleazer, Jr. (ed.), *American Junior Colleges* (Washington, D.C.: American Council on Education, 1964).

[2] Edmund J. Gleazer, Jr. (ed.), *Junior College Directory* (Washington, D.C.: American Association of Junior Colleges, 1961). This particular edition of *Junior College Directory* was used since it is the only one which enumerates faculty and administrative staff members separately.

the proportion of part-time teachers in such junior colleges tends to be high.

The second highest percentage of part-time staff members is claimed by the independent junior college: 35 per cent. The explanation for this rests in part on the sharing of the staff with a high school which is part of the total operation. A second factor playing a significant part is the number of technical institutes which use as part-time staff members employees of local industrial organizations.

The other three types of junior college, with the percentage of part-time staff members in each, are as follows: district, 31.2 per cent; church-related, 27.1 per cent; and state, 15.2 per cent. It is of interest that one reason for the large proportion of part-time staff members in the district junior colleges is their use of part-time personnel in their adult evening programs.

Part-time staff members in all five types of junior college number 12,882 (or about 40 per cent) out of a total of 35,902 full-time and part-time personnel.

When professional staff members of junior colleges are classified on the basis of sex, approximately 71 per cent are men and 29 per cent are women. This proportion varies when the individual types of junior college are concerned.

The type with the highest percentage of men is the state junior college, with 76.3 per cent. The other types, with the corresponding percentages of men are: local, 72.7 per cent; district, 74.2 per cent; church-related, 53.4 per cent; and independent, 67.9 per cent.

It will be seen from this listing that the church-related private junior college has the smallest percentage of men in the professional staff. Although no conclusive evidence is available to explain this circumstance, a probable explanation lies in the fact that professional staff salaries in a large number of Protestant denominational junior colleges are comparatively low, and existing differential in salaries for men and women would cause the positions with the lower-salaried positions to be filled by women.

Faculty

The preceding considerations have dealt with the professional staff as a whole, teachers and administrators. Attention now will be given to the instructional staff only. Two recent publications, one by Medsker[3] and one by Thornton[4] provide most of the data reported.

Medsker's study is based on questionnaire returns from 3274 faculty members in 74 junior colleges, representing all the types considered above. The report provides summary statements concerning (1) full-time status, (2) sex, (3) highest degree held, and (4) previous teaching experience. No effort will be made to compare Medsker's data with those already reported, for his are confined to the instructional staff only.

He reports that 68 per cent of the respondents to his inquiry were full-time faculty members, and 72 per cent were men. The distribution on the basis of the highest degree held was: doctorate, 9.6 per cent; master's, 64.6 per cent; and bachelor's, 17.0 per cent. He found that 6.7 per cent of those supplying information had no earned degree.[4a]

In his reference to the previous teaching experience of the junior college teachers included in his study, Medsker states:

> More than 64 per cent of the group had formerly taught in secondary or elementary schools or in both, mostly, however, in secondary schools. Almost half of the teachers in the local unified colleges [classified as *local public* in this study] had taught in secondary schools as had about a third of the staff in local separate districts [called *district* in this study]. Very few of the staff in state junior colleges and even fewer in extension centers [*branch public*] had had secondary school experience. The large number of teachers with experience at the secondary level confirms the general belief that high school teachers tend to move into the junior college. This is most likely to happen in unified systems where the central administration is empowered to make such transfers and where the staff is likely to regard the move as a promotion in status. The same progression occurs to a lesser degree in the local separate [*district*] junior colleges where teachers in nearby high schools are likely to apply for junior college positions.[5]

Thornton reports on working conditions in community junior colleges. Among the topics considered, three are selected for sum-

---

3 Leland L. Medsker, *The Junior College: Progress and Prospect* (New York: McGraw-Hill Book Company, 1964).

4 James W. Thornton, Jr., *The Community Junior College* (New York: John Wiley .& Sons, Inc., 1960).

4a Medsker, *op. cit.,* pp. 171–72.

5 *Ibid.,* p. 172.

mary here: (1) teaching load, (2) salaries, and (3) tenure and retirement.

Teaching loads. He reports that "teaching assignments in public junior colleges tend to approximate fifteen credit hours of teaching per semester."[6] He points out, however, that this figure is frequently deceptive when used as an index to clock hours. Teachers of laboratory courses may find themselves with a load exceeding twenty hours per week. In courses where the scheduled weekly hours exceed the credit hours, the teaching load will vary between sixteen and twenty clock hours.[7]

Salaries. On the topic of salaries, he states:

> In general, the data indicate that junior college teachers receive median salaries considerably higher than those of secondary teachers . . . and between the medians for college and university assistant professors and associate professors. . . .[8]

He reports also that median salaries for junior college teachers vary in relation to the section of the country in which the junior college is located. In descending order from the highest to the lowest median salary on the basis of geographical area, the order is: Far West, Middle Atlantic, Middle States, Southwest, Northwest, New England, and Southeast.[9]

A later report on salaries based on 483 public and nonpublic junior colleges approximates the same order with two exceptions; the Midwest trades places with the Middle Atlantic, and the Northwest with the Southwest. In this report the median salaries in each section are as follows: Far West, $8892; Midwest, $7829; Middle Atlantic, $7390; Northwest, $6572; Southwest, $6459; New England, $6290; and Southeast, $5804.[10]

Tenure and retirement. Thornton indicates that tenure is acquired by junior college teachers most often on the completion of a probationary period, which varies in length. Thus, teachers who are regularly re-employed annually during the probationary period, achieve tenure automatically when this probationary period is passed.[11]

---

[6] Thornton, *op. cit.,* pp. 137–38.

[7] *Ibid.*

[8] *Ibid.,* p. 139.

[9] *Ibid.,* p. 140.

[10] Ray C. Maul, "Are Junior College Salaries Competitive?" *Junior College Journal* 34:6 (March 1964), 22.

[11] Thornton, *op. cit.,* p. 140.

Most junior college teachers in public junior colleges share in the retirement benefits available to all public school teachers. Since Thornton's book concerned itself with community junior colleges, and since this term is most commonly applied to public junior colleges, he makes no comments on retirement programs in the private institutions.

Although practices vary in the private junior colleges, there are two which are fairly common. In the church-related junior colleges, many of the faculty members participate in retirement programs set up by the church which operates the junior college. Another fairly common practice is the shared-contribution plan, in which the teacher and the college participate in a program of purchasing annuities. Social security programs exist in both public and private junior colleges.

Teachers in both public and private junior colleges retire at a certain chronological age. Practices vary as to whether the retirement shall be compulsory when this age is reached.

Thornton gives some consideration to the practice of requiring teaching certificates for the instructional staff in public junior colleges as is required for teachers in public schools. He points out that such certification is required in only nine states: California, Florida, Illinois, Maryland, Michigan, Minnesota, New Jersey, Utah, and Washington.[12] In addition to the certification in these states, an almost universal requirement for employment in junior colleges is possession of the master's degree. Exceptions to this requirement are made occasionally, but never in large numbers except in vocational fields, where it is sometimes difficult to find teachers who meet the dual requirement of the master's degree and successful trade experience.

Although inveighed against in the earlier years of junior college development in the United States, the use of academic rank among the instructional staff is on the increase. In a report in *Junior College Journal* in March 1964, returns from 464 public and private junior colleges showed that 18.1 per cent used a system of academic rank in 1962. Returns from 483 junior colleges of both major divisions showed the percentage to have increased to 29.2 in 1964. These same returns show that the use of academic rank is growing

---

[12] *Ibid.*, p. 144.

more rapidly in public junior colleges than those in private ones. Based on the same two years, 1962 and 1964, the increase in public junior colleges was from 19.3 per cent to 32 per cent; in the private junior colleges, the increase was from 15.7 per cent to 23 per cent.[13]

Administrative Staff

Fewer definitive studies have been made of the characteristics of administrators in junior colleges. There is, however, a small amount of authoritative information that can be summarized.

One such body of information is contained in an article by Ray Hawk, who reports on seven characteristics of the chief administrator in 162 colleges, both public and private. The characteristics include:

(1) age upon assuming present position, (2) number of years in the position, (3) previous positions held, (4) highest degree earned, (5) principal field of academic specialization, (6) type of position predecessor took upon leaving, (7) length of time he served as head of the college.[14]

Hawk used the second of the listed characteristics, "number of years in the position," as a basis for identifying trends. In this study, however, the emphasis is on current status, so the portion of the article describing trends is not used.

Background. The average age of the 162 administrators at the time of taking office was 42.5 years.[15]

Seven, or 4.3 per cent of the administrators, had only a bachelor's degree. The master's degree was the highest held by 84, or 51.9 per cent. Earned doctorates were held by 71, or 43.8 per cent. In respect to the baccalaureate and master's degrees, the percentage is far below that of the professional staff as a whole, while the percentage with the doctorate far exceeded that of the total professional staff.[16]

The greatest number (49.4 per cent) of these administrators had their highest degree in education. In descending order, the other

---

[13] Maul, *Junior College Journal, op.* cit., p. 23.

[14] Ray Hawk, "A Profile of Junior College Presidents," *Junior College Journal,* 30:6 (February 1960), 340–46.

[15] *Ibid.,* p. 342.

[16] *Ibid.,* p. 343.

fields of specialization are: social science, 24.1 per cent; science, 13.6 per cent; humanities, 7.4 per cent; and others 5.5 per cent.[17]

One aspect of Hawk's study concerned previous positions held by the administrators before coming to their office. Those coming from a junior college staff position (not the presidency) were the most numerous: 24.1 per cent. Following close behind were two other positions, each with 21.6 per cent: (another) junior college presidency and public school administrator. Other positions include: four-year college staff, 19.1 per cent; ministry, 6.8 per cent; government or private foundations, 6.2 per cent; and industry, 0.6 per cent.[18]

Predecessors. Consideration was given to the question of the type of position taken by the immediate predecessor of the current incumbent. The sample was reduced to 151, for eleven of the presidents were in new junior colleges and had had no predecessors. Of the group 27.2 per cent had retired, and 7.3 per cent had died in office; 31.1 per cent had moved to other administrative positions in junior colleges, four-year colleges, or public schools. The remaining 34.4 per cent were distributed as follows: private business, 8.6 per cent; government or private foundations, 7.3 per cent; four-year college teaching staff, 6.6 per cent; another junior college position, 5.3 per cent; ministry, 4 per cent; and returned to graduate school, 2.6 per cent.[19]

The study revealed that the average tenure of the incumbents' predecessors was 10.3 years. When he compared these figures with other studies, Hawk concluded that the average tenure would be approximately ten years.[20]

Salaries. Morrison reported on administrative salaries in junior colleges in 1959–60. Three categories of administrators were included in the report: presidents, academic deans, and chief business officers. Data were based on returns from 146 junior colleges, ninety-four public and fifty-two private. The report also gave consideration to the size of enrollment in the junior colleges. Presidents in all public junior colleges had an average salary of $11,890, with a range of an average of $9270 in the smallest junior colleges (500

[17] *Ibid.,* p. 343.
[18] *Ibid.,* p. 345.
[19] *Ibid.,* p. 345.
[20] *Ibid.,* p. 345.

or fewer students) to an average of $16,340 in the largest junior colleges (2500 or more). The over-all average in the private junior colleges was $9800, with a range of $8960 to $14,160. The largest private junior colleges were in the 1000–2499 enrollment interval.[21]

Salaries for academic deans in all public and private junior colleges show a sharper contrast than salaries for presidents. The average salary for academic deans in all public junior colleges included in the sample is $10,600; for all private junior colleges, $6380. The range from the smallest public junior colleges to the largest is from $7250 to $12,960. Average salary for this office in private junior colleges is quoted for the interval of the smallest enrollment only (below 500), and is $5730.

Chief business officers in all public junior colleges received an average of $8310, and the range of averages from smallest to largest is $6600 to $11,500. The average for only the interval of the smallest enrollment in private junior colleges was reported $5910.

Summary

The characteristics of the professional staff of junior colleges described in this chapter are constantly changing. The data presented, however, enable one to gain a general understanding of some of the more significant aspects of the junior college staff.

---

[21] D. Grant Morrison, "Administrative Salaries in Junior Colleges," *Junior College Journal*, 32: 5 (January 1962), 260.

CHAPTER VI

Administrative Organization

The administrative organization of junior colleges, like all other characteristics of these educational institutions, varies widely. For purposes of analysis, it is possible to recognize certain similarities in clusters of junior colleges collected according to type. The method of selecting the junior college board illustrates this point.

Board members in local and district public junior colleges, for example, are usually elected by popular vote. Members for branch public and state junior colleges are usually appointed by an elected official. Church-related junior colleges board members most often are selected by religious communities, while boards of independent junior colleges usually are self-perpetuating.

Types of Junior Colleges

Because of the relationship of particular aspects of junior colleges to the major types of these institutions, it is desirable, as the first step in describing administrative organization, that the type be defined. Consideration was given in the first chapter to the two major divisions of junior colleges: public and private. Consideration will be given here to four types of public junior colleges, and three types of private junior colleges. In addition, some consideration will be given to a fourth type of private junior college.

Public. The first type of public junior college is the local. These junior colleges are the natural outgrowth of the upward extension of secondary schools. The school district which maintains the secondary school, whether it be a high school district or one that provides both elementary and high schools, merely adds another unit to its program, the junior college. Control over the junior college is exercised by the school district board, and the administrative head of the junior college reports to the superintendent of schools in the district.

Teachers in local public junior colleges frequently teach classes in both the high school and the junior college. In such instances, care is exercised in most cases to assign to college-level courses only those teachers who meet the accreditation standards for junior college teachers.

Junior colleges of this type often share with high schools the use of a common physical plant. The junior college, for example, may occupy a separate wing of the high school building, or it may be housed in a separate building or buildings on the same campus, with common use of such specialized facilities as laboratories, shops, or gymnasiums. In still other instances, the local junior college is completely separate from the high school.

The local public junior college is supported out of the general budget for the school district. This circumstance has led, in many instances, to attempts to remove the junior college from school district control to an independent status in a district of its own. Whether correctly or incorrectly, the protest has been made that, in times when curtailment of the budget is required, the junior college unit is first to feel the financial pinch. Moreover, those who protest point out that in matters of budget the junior college unit is constantly competing with at least one other unit, the high school, and very often with the elementary school, as well.

The upshot of such protests has been a gradual reduction of local junior colleges and their transformation into district institutions. California and Texas are two states in which these transformations have been frequent. Currently, local junior colleges are found in greatest numbers in the Midwestern states.

The district junior college, as indicated in the preceding paragraph, is found in a district organized solely for the maintenance of a junior college. These junior colleges have their own board, an exclusive source of income, and their own campus, physical plant, administrative organization, and faculty.

The principle element of difference among district junior colleges lies in the nature of the district. Some junior college districts have boundaries which are coterminous with those of an existing school district. Others are formed through the consolidation of two or more school districts. In some cases, the district boundaries are defined by those of a county. In others, district boundaries include two or more counties. Some district boundaries include those of school districts contiguous to each other but located in more than one county. The "district" of the district junior college, then, may vary. One of the reasons for the separate junior college district is to overcome the inadequate size of the district or districts used as units for schools of an elementary or secondary level.

A third type of public junior college is the branch of a public four-year college or a university. The control of a junior college of this type is vested in the board of the parent institution. The administrative head of the branch unit typically reports to an official of the parent institution who has been assigned the responsibility of coordinating the work of these educational institutions. Faculty appointments and curriculum organization are directly supervised through faculty channels in the parent institution.

The greatest number of junior colleges of this type are found in eight states: Alaska, Indiana, Oklahoma, Pennsylvania, Utah, Virginia, West Virginia, and Wisconsin. Two public universities in Indiana—Indiana University and Purdue University—prefer that their extension centers or "regional campuses" not be listed as branch junior colleges. Consequently, lists of junior colleges of more recent years omit them. In Alaska, Oklahoma, Pennsylvania, West Virginia, and Wisconsin, the junior colleges are branches of only one university in each state. The branch institutions in Oklahoma have developed a greater amount of autonomy than any of the similar institutions in the other states. West Virginia, in contrast to the other states, has only one branch junior college, Potomac State College of West Virginia University, located at Keyser.

Branch public junior colleges should not be confused with public junior colleges which are legally included in a state system of higher education. Examples of such systems are found in varying forms in such states as Arizona, Georgia, Massachusetts, New York, and Oregon. Oklahoma presents the interesting case of a parent university which is itself a part of such a system. The patterns of these state systems vary so widely that no attempt will be made to provide a description of them.

State junior colleges, the fourth type of public institution, proceeds on the same basis as other state-supported and state-controlled colleges and universities. Examples of this type of junior college may be found in eight states: Georgia, New Mexico, New York, North Dakota, Oklahoma, Oregon, Utah, and Vermont. As was pointed out earlier, control of these junior colleges is vested in appointed board or boards, and a substantial portion of their financial support is appropriated by state legislatures.

Private.   Church-related junior colleges constitute the most numerous type of private junior colleges. These junior colleges are controlled and operated by some religious group. With the exception of the preseminary Roman Catholic junior colleges, admission is not restricted to membership in the sponsoring religious group.

American Junior Colleges[1] lists 163 church-related colleges. Those sponsored by various religious orders and groups of the Roman Catholic Church number sixty-six, or slightly over two fifths of the total. Of the sixty-six institutions, forty-six are of the preseminary type and are not open to the lay public. Other religious denominations with ten or more junior colleges include the Baptist (twenty-six), Lutheran (ten), Methodist (twenty-eight), and Presbyterian (ten). Fifteen other denominations sponsor one or more junior colleges.

Church-related junior colleges receive their financial support from a number of sources, and policies concerning relative amounts from each source vary even among junior colleges of a given religious group. Among the more prominent of these sources are: returns on endowment funds, gifts and donations, subventions from the groups themselves, and, in most instances, tuition fees.

The independent junior colleges, as was indicated in Chapter I, were created, in the main, by gifts from philanthropic groups or individuals. Their number was increased by the transformation of a number of proprietary junior colleges which were rechartered as nonprofit organizations. The distinctive characteristic of these junior colleges is expressed in the name of the type; independent. These organizations are completely independent of religious organizations and, except for the charter issued by the state in which they operate, they are independent of public control.

One additional type of private junior college should be mentioned, although the total number is very small and is gradually becoming smaller: the junior college which is controlled and operated by nonpublic, nondenominational groups. One of these groups is the Young Mens' Christian Association, which currently

---

1 Edmund J. Gleazer, Jr. (ed.), *American Junior Colleges,* 6th ed. (Washington, D.C.: American Council on Education, 1964).

operates four junior colleges. The other organization of this description is the P.E.O. Sisterhood, which operates one junior college: Cottey College, at Nevada, Missouri.

Two junior colleges listed in *American Junior Colleges*[2] parallel the branch public junior colleges. These two educational institutions are branches of privately controlled colleges but, aside from this feature, are subject to the same description as the branch public junior colleges.

The point was made at the outset of this chapter that such similarities as might be found in the administration organizational patterns occurred among the clusters of institutions collected under the several types of junior college. In deference to space restrictions, however, and in an effort to eliminate duplication, the picture of the administrative organization will be drawn in broad terms, with only general reference to the influence of a particular type of junior college.

Junior College Boards

Junior colleges, like other institutions of higher education, are controlled by boards. These boards are usually made up of non-educators, and contain several observable variables. One variable concerns the number of members making up the board.

The number of board members rarely is less than five, but the maximum number may run to forty or fifty or more. Generally speaking, the smaller boards will be found in the public institutions; the larger boards, in the private ones. If the number of board members is large, provision is usually made for a subgroup to be designated as an executive committee and empowered to act for the board as a whole.

Election to board membership generally follows one of three patterns: election, appointment, and co-option. Local and district public junior college boards members, like those of church-related junior colleges, are usually chosen by public election. The electorate is restricted to the geographical area (district or congregation) within which the junior college operates. Members of branch public and state junior colleges are usually appointed to their offices by some governmental official or agency, although in some states they

---

[2] *Ibid.*

are elected. The practice of co-option, or selection by the board itself, is found almost exclusively among the independent junior colleges.

Internal Administration

The administrative structure of junior colleges generally follows that found in most colleges and universities. The chief administrative officer in all but the local public and the branch public junior colleges reports directly to the board. In the local public college, this official, usually called *dean* or *director*, reports to the superintendent of schools, who (in some instances) assumes the dual administrative title of *superintendent of schools* and *president of the junior college*. As was explained, the chief administrative officer of the branch public junior college, in most cases called a *director*, reports directly to a coordinator of the off-campus program. Exceptions to this will be found in a few of the states involved.

In the administrative organization, on the levels below the chief administrative officers, the three major divisions of the junior college are recognized: faculty and curriculum, students, and business. Appropriate titles for these divisions will usually be found, although the assignment of administrative responsibility often is highly incongruous with that normally expected by the nature of the three divisions.

Among the areas in which incongruities frequently occur are those of selection of professional staff (especially teachers), budget-making, and the direction of the student-personnel program. This last-named function is frequently placed at a level lower than that of the academic dean and the business manager. In many junior colleges, the responsibility for administrative supervision of the student-personnel program will not be assigned, thus preventing the needed coordination.

All types of junior colleges are involved in the description and criticism advanced in the preceding paragraphs. From the descriptive standpoint, however, it should be noted that church-related junior colleges will have one administrative official usually not found in the other types. This official is the college chaplain or college pastor. His administrative assignment, in addition to the responsibility implied in his title, is usually in the division of student-personnel services and is usually concerned with guidance and counseling. Occasionally, he works also in the field of public relations.

The preceding paragraphs depict the administrative organization in very broad terms, but they should suffice to give a general idea of the organizational pattern.

CHAPTER VII

Plant and Finance

The volume to which reference has been made many times, *American Junior Colleges,* was produced on the basis of data supplied by individual junior colleges. Included in the questionnaire items were requests for total current gross income, value of campus and plant, and number of acres included in the campus. The figures supplied were for the academic year, 1961–62.

Physical Plant

The figures supplied by the several junior colleges who responded to this request (approximately 85 per cent of the 655 "Institutional Exhibits" contained in the volume) give a rough idea of the gross income, value of plant and campus, and campus acreage in 1961–62. The total for current gross income for the academic year was, $399,962,000; the value of grounds and plant was $389,-842,000; the acreage was 77,288. If estimates were added for the approximately one hundred junior colleges which did not supply data, it is not unreasonable to suppose that the income and value figures would each approach a half-billion dollars. The figure for acreage would increase, although probably not nearly so much, for many of the junior colleges not responding to this item were located in cities where the high price of real estate would work against large campuses for the junior colleges.

Figures are not currently available to indicate the gross appreciation in the value of junior college physical plants since the conclusion of World War II, but there is little doubt that they would reveal a phenomenal increase. This estimate is based on two factors (1) the substantial increase in the number of new junior colleges established, and (2) the marked expansion of the physical plants of existing junior colleges in all sections of the country and, in many instances, the construction of completely new plants. Expansion of the physical facilities of junior colleges has kept pace with all the other features in which material gains have been noted.

The report of increases must not be mistakenly applied to all the junior colleges. Nor should the conclusion be reached that there is a rapid elimination of the instances mentioned in Chapter VI, in which junior colleges are housed in the same building with high schools. Junior colleges which are housed in the same buildings as high schools, or are on the same grounds with or without cooperative use of certain specialized facilities, operate in a manner consistent with a long-held policy of extending the secondary schools upward. Moreover, in nearly all such cases, there is a wide acceptance of the idea that the junior college functions best when it is part of the local school district.

Many private junior colleges, both church-related and independent, set a figure to represent the optimum number of students to be served, and hold to this figure. Although this will often require modest expansion of physical plant and facilities, it does not involve the necessity for marked increase in capacity.

Expansions of the physical plant, whether they be modest or large, show the adaptation of many advances in building materials and design, and the application of advances in electronics. There is in this some evidence of more functional planning, and the emergence and use of architectural firms that specialize in designing buildings for educational services. The time when the junior college buildings could be identified by their standard design is disappearing.

One aspect of the physical plant and facilities which has influenced the development of the curriculum is found in the relatively high cost of vocational education. The only phases of the academic program which even approach this cost factor are science, which needs laboratories, and possibly foreign languages, which now need language laboratories. Over a longer span of time, however, the vocational program is more costly because the equipment rapidly becomes obsolete.

The initial costs of technical shops or business education departments are high. In the case of business education, the increasing popularity of data-processing programs has increased the previously not inconsequential costs tremendously. Even if a junior college can justify the initial cost, the rapid progress made in developing new machines can easily make obsolete the equipment in many of the vocational shops.

These cost factors cannot be ignored. The answer to this question of providing vocational programs must take them into consideration. When such consideration is given, many junior college boards and administrators are forced to acknowledge that, no matter how urgent the need for the vocational program may appear, it cannot be developed fully in the junior college because of prohibitively high costs.

As junior college enrollments increase in certain sections of the country, students are drawn from a constantly widening geographical area. This circumstance has led to the addition of residence halls to the physical plant of some junior colleges and to the increase in the capacity of residence halls in others. The addition of residence halls or the increase in capacity of existing ones, in many cases, are financed by the sale of self-liquidating bonds underwritten by the federal government. This procedure has also simplified the expansion of dining halls, cafeterias, and student union buildings. Anticipated revenues are pledged as collateral for the interest and redemption.

Financing

The preceding paragraph indicates one of the many ways in which junior colleges are financed. In this particular example, the method of financing is available to both public and private junior colleges. Many other aspects of financing, however, are available only to one major division or the other.

The finances for operating junior colleges and providing the capital outlay come principally from seven sources: (1) legislative appropriations, (2) loans, (3) gifts, (4) grants, (5) investments, (6) tuition fees, and (7) taxes. In a very real sense, all these sources are relied upon by both private and public institutions.

Legislative appropriations. Appropriations from the state legislature are used to support both current operations and capital outlay. Twice as many states, however, provide funds for current operations as do for capital construction. Martorana[1] identifies twenty-

---

[1] S. V. Martorana, "The Legal Status of American Junior Colleges," in Edmund Gleazer, Jr. (ed.), *American Junior Colleges*, 6th ed. (Washington, D.C.: American Council on Education, 1964), pp. 40, 42.

eight states (of the thirty-eight that have junior college legislation) as having legislative appropriations to help support current operating costs, with fourteen providing such assistance for capital construction.

It requires a loose interpretation of the term *appropriations* to include church-related junior colleges as recipients of such financial assistance. It is a matter of fact, however, that many institutions of this type do receive financial assistance as a result of decisions made by the legislative bodies of churches.

Loans. Borrowing money, almost always for capital outlay, is a common practice among all types of junior college. Practices vary as to the regulations governing such securing of funds. In nearly all instances, the borrowing is effected through the sale of bonds. Reference has already been made to the use of self-liquidating bonds underwritten by the federal government for use in constructing revenue-producing buildings such as dormitories, dining halls, and student unions.

As was indicated, borrowing is, in essence, limited to obtaining capital funds for construction projects. Borrowing money for current operating expenses, except in cases of temporary emergencies, is not regarded as justifiable.

Gifts and grants. Although gifts provide a source of financial support for all types of junior college, the three types of private junior college described previously rely on this source much more than the four types of public junior college. For many of these private junior colleges, gifts—along with student tuition and fees—constitute the source of by far the greatest portion of their income. Fund-raising, through the solicitation of gifts, often is one of the most important administrative tasks of the presidents of private junior colleges, and their success in this position is likely to be judged by their success in this undertaking.

Gifts are sought from many sources, but are secured primarily from four sources: (1) alumni, individuals, or groups, (2) churches —for church-related colleges, often on the basis of special collections, (3) foundations, and (4) philanthropists—wealthy individuals or families who develop a personal interest in a college.

Junior colleges, like four-year colleges or universities, occasionally receive grants from governmental agencies or foundations to make special studies.

Investments.   Many junior colleges, especially the private types, derive a portion of their income from the returns on investments. These investments usually are carried in the form of endowments, in which the capital funds are used only for reinvestment. The college often uses a committee of the board as its investment agency. Sometimes this service is secured from an investment counselor not connected with the institution. Because of the low returns on investments, endowment is not relied upon nearly so much as in the past. Many junior colleges have come to place greater reliance on gifts given regularly over the years. The use of returns on investments as a source of income is almost exclusively restricted to private junior colleges. It is a source involving few public junior colleges.

Student fees.   Student fees serve as a source of income in all types of junior college, but not in all junior colleges. In eight states —California, Colorado, Illinois, Kansas, Mississippi, Missouri, Pennsylvania, and Wisconsin—from one to all the public junior colleges charge no tuition. In some of these junior colleges, however, special fees are collected from the students. It should be noted that these special fees do not serve as a subterfuge for elimination of tuition charges, for such special fees are charged in many junior colleges which also charge tuition fees.

Student fees fall into several categories, the most frequent of which are: tuition, special fees for all students, special fees for certain subjects (as in the case of certain branches of the fine arts), and room and board charges in junior colleges which provide these services.

In general, tuition fees are lowest in local or district junior colleges, and highest in the independent institution. Church-related junior colleges rank next highest to independent institutions. As in all other phases of the junior college, the wide variance in practices makes such generalizations of doubtful value.

Local and district junior colleges often assess tuition fees on the basis of residence. For example, students living in the legally defined district served by the junior college will pay one tuition rate; those living in the state, but not in the district, will pay a higher rate; while those living outside the state will pay a much higher rate. The rationale underlying these differentiated rates is based on the fact that local taxes are collected in the district to support the junior college, and state legislative appropriations help in the financial support. Tuition rates are thus geared to these conditions. Branch and state junior colleges charge higher tuition rates for out-of-state students than for state residents.

Taxes. Finally, a common feature of the local school district of which some junior colleges are a part, and of the district junior colleges, is their local taxing power. The methods of computing, collecting, and turning over the taxes varies considerably from one section of the country to another. In all sections, however, the conditions underlying the taxing power is the same. Certain taxes earmarked exclusively for the junior college are levied and collected in the area in which the school is located, and become available to the institution.

Private junior colleges participate in this source in another way. Although taxes are not levied in their behalf, most of them benefit from the fact that their property is tax-exempt. This exemption makes possible the use of funds that would otherwise be paid out as taxes for other junior college costs.

All four types of public junior college—local, district, branch, and state—benefit financially from appropriations of state legislatures. Although this statement applies to all four types, it is not true in all the states in which are to be found examples of the local and district junior colleges. Branch public and state junior colleges are designated, by definition, as recipients of such assistance. As with almost all aspects of the junior college, appropriation practices vary from state to state.

CHAPTER VIII

Junior College Standards

The quality of the performance of junior colleges, as of all other types of educational institutions, is measured by various evaluative devices. Consideration has already been given to one of these devices in Chapter V, in the discussion of certification practices for teachers and administrators in public junior colleges. This chapter will consider two other sets of standards: those that must be met in the establishment of new public junior colleges of the local and district type, and those imposed by the several types of accrediting agencies.

Standards for Establishment

The creation of new local and district public junior colleges most often depends on local initiative. Because local initiative cannot always be depended on to match the enthusiasm for the project with the assurance of the elements necessary for providing a sound educational program, safeguards in the form of predetermined standards are imposed, usually by some state agency.

Although there is no uniformity in regard to the nature of these standards, certain general features will be found in most instances. Martorana has summarized these:

> . . . there are two basic stipulations commonly required for legal establishment of a public junior college. These are indications of (1) the potential size of the institution and (2) the potential basis for financing its operation.[1]

He further points out that the lack of agreement on precise standards relating to these two factors indicates an uncertainty as to just how they should be measured.

Procedures. The first step in the establishment of a junior col-

---

[1] S. V. Martorana, "The Legal Status of American Public Junior Colleges," Edmund Gleazer, Jr. (ed.), in *American Junior Colleges,* 6th ed. (Washington, D.C.: American Council on Education, 1964), pp. 37–39.

lege is usually taken by the submission of a petition from the locality desiring the junior college. This petition is addressed to the state agency empowered to act on such requests, and is followed by a survey of the locality to ascertain whether it measures up to the standards required. "Measuring up" may be manifested by a minimum population in the proposed district, or by a specified minimum enrollment in the secondary schools. Ability to support the junior college will frequently be determined on the basis of a specified minimum tax evaluation.

The examiner, often an affiliate of the state agency which deals with such matters, may study other aspects of the community which would be regarded as necessary prerequisites for the establishment of a new junior college. His report is submitted to the state agency, frequently a state board associated with the educational services in a state. This agency or board, after studying the report, will pass judgment on the original petition. Granting the petition often takes the form of permitting a local election to be called to determine the will of the electorate on the proposal to establish the junior college.

The description of the steps taken in the establishment of a new junior college follows generally the procedure used in one state. Its similarity to procedures used in other states, however, enables it to convey a general idea of what is done.

There is a great likelihood that junior colleges, both public and private, will be relied upon more and more to carry heavier loads of the increasing number of prospective candidates for a program of higher education. If this be the case, there is one standard for establishing new junior colleges that needs much greater consideration than it is now being given in most states. This is a standard to assure that public junior colleges are established in the strategic centers over the state to enable them to be of maximum service.

Attention should be given to the belief, entertained by many, that junior colleges should not be established within a specified distance of existing institutions of higher education. This belief has validity only if the existing institution is actually serving satisfactorily the students who would be served by the junior college, and at a cost as low as that which would be charged by the junior college.

Accrediting Agencies

The second aspect of standards concerns those which are established by the several types of accrediting agencies. Some of these agencies deal with both public and private junior colleges, while others restrict their service to only one or the other of the two major divisions. In general, these standards provide a means of evaluating the quality of a junior college actually in operation, rather than prior to its establishment. The accrediting agencies include some six general types: (1) state departments of education, (2) state universities, (3) legally established state commissions, (4) voluntary associations, (5) professional organizations, and (6) regional agencies.

State departments of education. One of the responsibilities assigned to state departments of education, or to organizations performing equivalent functions but carrying different names, is the supervision of the certification of teachers for the public schools of the respective states. This responsibility includes not only checking on applications to see that all regulations have been met, but extends also to the matter of examining the teacher education program of all colleges and universities in a state to be sure that these programs are consistent with predetermined standards. It is on this basis that this state agency becomes, in a very real sense, an accrediting agency.

In the hierarchy of accrediting agencies, considered on the basis of the comprehensiveness of the standards and the rigorousness of their application, the state department frequently occupies the lowest echelon. For this reason, many newly established junior colleges obtain this recognition first, as they are in the process of preparing to meet the higher standards of other accrediting organizations. Hence, in the matter of recognition, accreditation by a state department of education carries the least significance.

State universities. During the years when junior colleges were first coming into prominence, recognition of their having attained satisfactory standards was accorded by state universities. Recognition was accorded through a simple agreement in which the state university accepted, at full value, credits earned in a junior college. Incidentally, in these earlier years, similar recognition was accorded by colleges and universities other than the state university. The recognition gained significance in the fact that, if the state university would accept credits earned in a junior college in the state, colleges and universities elsewhere would extend the same recognition to transfer students.

The task of accrediting junior colleges involved much extra work for the state university, and also involved a certain element of politics. For these reasons, many state universities have been eager to shed this responsibility. This accounts for the steady reduction in the list of universities engaged in this undertaking. Currently, accreditation from this source is available in very few states.

State commissions.   Several states have created, through legislative action, organizations charged with the responsibility of imposing standards as a basis for recognition of junior colleges. The nature and the purposes of these organizations vary widely from state to state. Their only elements of similarity are their creation by legal action, and their evaluative responsibility for junior colleges. The following are representative of this type of agency: the Iowa Committee on Secondary School and College Relations, the Massachusetts Board of Collegiate Authority, the Michigan Commission on College Accreditation, the Mississippi Commission on College Accreditation, and the North Carolina College Conference.

Voluntary associations.   The state of Texas provides an example of another type of accrediting agency, the voluntary association, called the Association of Texas Colleges and Universities. This organization differs from those described in the preceding paragraph in that it is nonpublic. Its membership is made up of four-year colleges, junior colleges, and universities, both public and private. Its published standards constitute the qualifications which must be met as a basis for membership. Separate standards exist for junior colleges.

Professional organizations.   Various professional groups have, for many years, made a practice of exercising an accrediting function. One of these, whose standards are applicable to technical programs in junior colleges, is the Engineer's Council for Professional Development. The specialized nature of the standards assures greater consideration for the technical phase of the junior college curriculum than is provided by the general agencies of accreditation. For this reason, this type of recognition is of greater significance than that of the general agencies.

Regional agencies. The highest form of recognition attainable by junior colleges is membership in a regional accrediting association. These associations, like the voluntary associations, are non-public in the sense that they are not agencies of the state or federal government. Standards imposed by these organizations constitute the qualifications for membership.

The regional associations, as their name implies, are made up of four-year colleges, junior colleges, universities, and high schools in a geographical region. Their membership includes both public and private junior colleges. Currently there are six of these associations: the Middle States Association of Colleges and Secondary Schools, the New England Association of Colleges and Secondary Schools, the North Central Association of Colleges and Secondary Schools, the Northwest Association of Secondary and Higher Schools, the Southern Association of Colleges and Schools, and the Western Association of Schools and Colleges. Although the regions vary in their geographical size, the North Central with nineteen states, and the Southern with eleven states are by far the largest.

Professional activity in the regional associations has always comprised far more than just that of investigating the qualifications of colleges and secondary schools applying for admission. All types of problems common to colleges and secondary schools are studied by the standing commissions and by special committees appointed for such work. Thus, although admission to membership does constitute the highest form of accreditation which junior colleges can attain, at the same time membership brings junior college leaders into association with other leaders of all types of institution in professional activities of concern to their common efforts.

Currently, approximately 60 per cent of the junior colleges have the highest form of recognition attainable: regional accreditation. Another 13 per cent have an intermediate level of accreditation: that accorded by state commission, voluntary association, state university, or professional. The remaining 27 per cent have attained the first level of recognition: that accorded by the state department of education.

It might be concluded that with well over a fourth of the junior colleges having attained only the first level of accreditation, there are many junior colleges which are not concerned with maintaining high standards. Such a conclusion would be incorrect. For example, many of the 27 per cent noted in the preceding paragraph are new institutions, too young to make application for membership in the regional accrediting association. The age factor operates in some regional agencies through a standard which requires the successful performance in a four-year college of transfer students from three graduating classes. If the new junior college enrolls only freshmen its first year, it will be two years before it has its first graduating class, two more years before it has three such classes, and an additional year before the performance record of its third class could be compiled.

Before leaving consideration of junior college accreditation, one other species of controls should be examined. In many of the states, some supervision and coordination of junior colleges is provided by a designated state agency. The nature of the supervision, like all other aspects of junior colleges, varies to a considerable extent. One aspect of this control exists in those states in which legislative appropriations, made on the basis of some formula, help to finance the junior colleges. Some species of supervision becomes necessary to assure that the stipulations of the formula are satisfied.

It would be a mistake to confuse this type of supervisory control with genuine accreditation, which relies upon the satisfaction of certain standards. But when formulas for state aid require documentary evidence as a basis for proving compliance, then the stipulations imposed do constitute a set of standards which must be met. In the same sense, the state agencies assigned responsibility for enforcement of the stipulations may be regarded as being a species of accrediting agency.

Finally, one aspect of the membership of junior colleges in professional organizations which do no accrediting should be noted. Of the 694 junior colleges listed in the 1964 *Junior College Directory,* 531, or over three fourths, were members of the American Association of Junior Colleges. Many of the junior colleges which are members announce this fact in their college catalogs. It should be understood that this Association is not an accrediting agency. A large number of junior colleges also belong to the regional associations of junior colleges. These associations are not accrediting agencies, and should not be confused with the regional association of colleges and secondary schools.

CHAPTER IX

The Place of the Junior College
in the United States

The material presented in Chapter I dealt with the relation of junior colleges to higher education in the United States. This chapter focuses attention on the junior college as a factor in the education of young people. Occasionally, discrepancies will be observed between figures cited earlier and figures appearing in this chapter. Such discrepancies arise because the figures are based on data collected at different times. Material presented earlier and new material are combined to provide a complete picture of junior colleges in the United States.

Much of the material used in describing the present status of junior colleges is taken from *Junior College Directory*.[1] In case other sources are used, they will be identified.

The Past and the Present

The junior colleges is completely native to the United States. Although it has been exported to other countries, its nature has been little influenced by educational institutions in other countries. Perhaps the fact that it is native to the United States accounts for the circumstance that junior colleges are found in every state in the nation (except one: Nevada), and in the Canal Zone, the District of Columbia, Puerto Rico, and the Virgin Islands.

The junior college is not a phenomenon popular in only one section of the country. Evidence of its nationwide popularity may be seen in listings of the first ten states on the basis of the number of junior colleges, and the first ten on the basis of enrollment. The first ten states in the order of number of junior colleges are: California (76), New York (66), Texas (46), Illinois (40), Pennsyl-

---

[1] Edmund Gleazer, Jr. (ed.), *Junior College Directory 1964*. (Washington, D.C.: American Association of Junior Colleges, 1964).

vania (34), Florida (32), Mississippi (27), Massachusetts (25), Iowa (21), and North Carolina (20). Ranked on the basis of enrollment, the order is: California (390,610), New York (68,829), Illinois (51,206), Texas (44,045), Florida (40,927), Michigan (39,827), Washington (26,797), Pennsylvania (19,983), Massachusetts (17,804), and Missouri (13,347). An examination of these lists shows that every major geographical section of the nation is represented.

Enrollment and staff. Total enrollment in the junior colleges, as of October 1963, was 902,584. Of this number, 789,294 were enrolled in public junior colleges, and 113,290 in private junior colleges. Full-time students in all junior colleges numbered 390,000; 259,033 were freshmen, 122,534 were sophomores, and 8433 were unclassified. Part-time students in junior colleges numbered 425,190, with 216,464 freshmen, 70,843 sophomores, and 137,883 unclassified. The large number of unclassified part-time students reflects the extensive group of adult students who enroll in courses but have no intention of completing college requirements.

A total of 41,263 full-time and part-time administrative and instructional staff members were employed in 694 junior colleges as of October 1963. Public junior colleges accounted for 33,010 of these staff members, while 8253 were on the staffs of private junior colleges. As of the date listed, there were 422 public junior colleges and 272 private junior colleges.

Distribution. Junior colleges of the seven types described in Chapter VI are found in all sections of the country. It is of interest, however, that some types tend to be concentrated in certain geographical areas. Local public junior colleges, for example, are found in large numbers in the Midwestern states; district junior colleges, in the West and Southwest. The largest number of branch public junior colleges are in Pennsylvania and Wisconsin. State junior colleges are found in many sections, but very few in the West. Church-related junior colleges are concentrated in the South and Southeast, and independent junior colleges in the East.

The turning of attention to concentrations of types of junior colleges in certain areas of the United States leads normally to the matter of the status of junior colleges in the several states. Since World War II, there have been significant developments.

As was pointed out in Chapter I, the period since World War II has witnessed a phenomenal increase in college enrollments in this country. Because control of public higher education rests with the individual states, there has been a great deal of concern in the states over the question of how best to accommodate the continuing increase of college students. This has led many states to reassess the role which junior colleges can play in carrying part of the increasing load. Not all the states which have faced this problem have assigned a heavier responsibility to junior colleges, but many have.

Alaska, for example, has five public junior colleges, all of which were established in 1954 or later. Arizona has doubled its number of junior colleges, and is anticipating a further increase. California, though in the junior college field since 1910, has given them a more rigorously defined status, and has created fifteen new public junior colleges since 1954. Florida has committed itself to vastly increased reliance on junior colleges of the twenty-eight public junior colleges in that state in October 1963, twenty-four were created in 1954 or later—eleven of these since 1959. Eight of the twelve junior colleges in Maryland came into existence in 1957 or later. The establishment of several public junior colleges in Massachusetts, in one sense, marks a reversal of state policy which has long favored the financing of higher education through nonpublic sources.

The states listed are examples of the reawakened interest in junior colleges and, in some cases, of the new interest in these institutions. The list, though, is far from complete. Legislation favorable to the development of junior colleges has been enacted in many other states. Among these are Michigan, Missouri, Illinois, New York, North Carolina, and Texas. It can be said with complete accuracy that, as state commissions and legislatures study plans for accommodating increases in college enrollments, junior colleges have been given an increasingly prominent place.

When studies of junior colleges have been made by states, the focus has been on public junior colleges. It would be a serious error to conclude from this that private junior colleges have ceased to grow in numbers. Although their increase has not matched that of the public junior colleges, the 1964 *Junior College Directory* lists fifty-eight private junior colleges that were created in 1954 or later. This represents 21.3 per cent of all the private junior colleges in existence in October 1963.

One reason for the slower increase of private junior colleges, in addition to the comparatively slower rate at which new institutions are created, is the transformation of such junior colleges into four-year colleges. In the four years elapsing between the publication of the fifth and sixth editions of *American Junior Colleges* (1960–64) thirty-one junior colleges became four-year colleges. Of this number, thirteen were church-related and six independent junior colleges.

Although private junior colleges do not receive the consideration that is given to public junior colleges in planning for higher education at the state level, there is no question as to the service they provide. In six states, enrollment in private junior colleges exceeds that in the public institutions. The states with the percentage of the total junior college enrollment represented by enrollments in private junior colleges are: Connecticut (87.9), Massachusetts (74.3), New Jersey (81.7), North Carolina (64.2), Pennsylvania (56.3), and Virginia (66.5). In ten other states, and the District of Columbia, there are no public junior colleges. These states are Alabama, Delaware, Hawaii, Louisiana, Maine, New Hampshire, Rhode Island, South Carolina, South Dakota, Tennessee, and the District of Columbia.

As states give more consideration to the role of public junior colleges in helping to accommodate the increasing number of students, recommended plans are developed which eventually get to the state legislature for action. That action has been taken is evidenced by Martorana's[2] report that, at the close of the legislative year in 1962, only twelve states had not passed general enabling legislation for the creation of junior colleges. These states are distributed throughout the United States, and some have enacted such legislation since 1962.

State legislatures have enacted laws dealing with many other aspects of junior college operation. For example, all the thirty-eight states whose legislatures have enacted laws pertaining to junior colleges have assigned responsibility for supervising and coordinating junior colleges; thirty-four now list prescribed prerequisites and

---

2 S. V. Martorana, "The Legal Status of American Public Junior Colleges, in Edmund Gleazer (ed.), *American Junior Colleges,* 6th ed. (Washington, D.C.: American Council on Education, 1964), pp. 31–47. The following report on the status of legislation pertaining to junior colleges is obtained from this source.

procedures for establishing public junior colleges; twenty-nine have provided for state financial aid to public junior colleges to defray their costs of current operation; and fourteen have provided state financial aid to junior colleges for capital construction. Some idea of the magnitude of the legislation may be gained from the fact that in the four-year period 1959–62, 124 legislative enactments were made.

Prospects for the Future

What is the future of the junior college in the United States? This interesting question has frequently come up in conferences which have concerned themselves with higher education in general, or junior colleges in particular. Though this educational institution has established itself solidly, there are still many people who view it with alarm or regard it as an unwanted ·interloper among the more dignified institutions of higher education—a pariah, an untouchable flaunting its shoddiness in a realm of respectability.

This opposition is fighting a losing battle. The loss can be predicted with complete accuracy, because opposition to junior colleges rests on ignorance of facts. The fact that junior colleges have penetrated all sections of the country is enough to indicate that they will be successful in this contest. At best, the opposition can hope only to fight a delaying action, a fight they are making in some states.

The inevitability of the continued growth of the junior college is grounded in its origin and past development. Although its roots run deeper, it is essentially the product of the vast social changes of the twentieth century. As this change has accelerated, the speed of growth and development of junior colleges has kept pace. Quantitatively, its future is assured.

From a qualitative standpoint, there has never been any doubt about the soundness of junior college programs. Evidence of a very convincing nature indicates that this will continue to be true. The 1964 *Junior College Directory* reports that 59.1 per cent of the junior colleges in the United States are accredited by regional accrediting associations. When it is observed that another 13.8 per cent of the junior colleges in existence in October 1963 had been established in 1960 or later, and hence had not had time to be accredited, only slightly over one fourth of all the junior colleges are not accounted for.[3]

Cognizance has already been given to the junior college's position in the evolving nature of higher education. Specialization in four-year colleges has been seen in most cases to begin with the third or junior year. It was pointed out that already in one state, a state university has been established in which the beginning year is the third. Because this action is consistent with the evolution taking place in higher education, it may be anticipated that other changes of this nature will follow.

Even though only one state university of the type described has been created, and even though it may be a long time before others come into existence, the junior college is already performing for thousands of students the educational service customarily found in the first and second years of the undergraduate program. It is logical to predict that this service will be provided for a continually increasing number of students in the future.

The junior college of the future will continue to exercise the transfer function, as it has done in the past. At the same time, however, there will be a sharp increase in programs of technical education for so-called terminal students. Many junior colleges have already entered this curricular field; many, many more will do so.

Public junior colleges and some private junior colleges will expand their programs in adult education and community service. The demand for these services has long existed. Many junior colleges have already developed programs which go far in satisfying these demands. The vacuum created by unsatisfied educational demands in many localities will be filled either by junior colleges or other agencies. The trend is definitely in the direction of fulfillment by junior colleges.

Private junior colleges will continue as an integral and significant part of the junior college movement. Those which are most successful as junior colleges will possess two characteristics: (1) a commitment to the junior college movement as the field in which their future lies, and (2) equal commitment to institutional purposes which go beyond being merely competitors of public junior colleges.

The junior colleges, especially those termed public, will become

---

[3] Gleazer, *Junior College Directory, op. cit.*

even more integral a part of the state system of higher education. A very few states will retain them as branches of the state university; an even smaller number will retain them as state junior colleges; but a substantial majority of the states will see them operated as district junior colleges, free of tuition charges. Financial support will come from taxes collected in the district, and from legislatively appropriated funds.

In the states, junior colleges will be established in predetermined regions to serve all high school graduates. The establishment of these junior colleges will work contrary to the principle underlying high school consolidation. Instead of several junior colleges being consolidated into one, need areas in the state for junior colleges will be identified and new junior colleges will be established there.

The future for junior colleges, public and private, is bright. It is to be hoped that progress toward this future will be steady, and on sound foundations.

Bibliography

Bogue, Jesse Parker, *The Community College*. New York: McGraw-Hill Book Company, 1950.

Campbell, Doak S., *A Critical Study of the Stated Purposes of the Junior College*. Nashville, Tenn.: George Peabody College for Teachers, 1930.

Clark, Burton R., *The Open Door College: A Case Study*. New York: McGraw-Hill Book Company, 1960.

Fields, Ralph R., *The Community College Movement*. New York: McGraw-Hill Book Company, 1962.

Gleazer, Edmund J., Jr. (ed.), *American Junior Colleges, 1960*. Washington, D.C.: American Council on Education, 1960.

Junior College Directory, 1964. Washington, D.C.: American Association of Junior Colleges, 1964.

Junior College Directory, 1963. Washington, D.C.: American Association of Junior Colleges, 1963.

Koos, Leonard Vincent, *The Junior College*. Minneapolis: The University of Minnesota, 1924.

———, *The Junior College Movement*. Boston: Ginn & Company, 1925.

Martorana, S. V., "The Legal Status of American Public Junior Colleges," *American Junior Colleges*. Washington, D.C.: American Council on Education, 1960.

Medsker, Leland L., *The Junior College: Progress and Prospect*. New York: McGraw-Hill Book Company, 1960.

Reynolds, James W., "Junior Colleges," *Encyclopedia of Educational Research*, 3rd ed. New York: The Macmillan Company, 1960.

Index

Index